A MILLION PIECES
- Most of them Missing

OrangeBooks Publication

1st Floor, Rajhans Arcade, Mall Road, Kohka, Bhilai, Chhattisgarh 490020

Website:**www.orangebooks.in**

© Copyright, 2023, Author

All rights reserved. No part of this book may be reproduced, stored in a retrieval system, or transmitted, in any form by any means, electronic, mechanical, magnetic, optical, chemical, manual, photocopying, recording or otherwise, without the prior written consent of its writer.

First Edition, 2023

A MILLION PIECES
MOST OF THEM MISSING

SANTHOSH NAMBALLA

OrangeBooks Publication
www.orangebooks.in

To

With love and Gratitude
Santhosh N

Foreword

There are a million pieces of each of us floating around, in this world. Find one and if you couldn't hold on to that one, find another. But this time, make sure you don't lose it.

Acknowledgements

To the very few people who believed in me even when I couldn't, this work is dedicated to you all.

Swathi Nadipineni (faculty from my college days), always indebted.

I now believe that there is always a woman (at the least, one) behind a man's work.

Thanks to

My under graduate roomies, forever soulmates, Sridhar and Pradeep. And Bhaskar Rao sir, my school principal who forced me through those English grammar classes.

Sir, I'm sure you would like me to have vast vocabulary in my armour but I always fall short of words when it comes to explaining how grateful I'm for every grammar class that you forced us to attend.

Special thanks to

My parents. Had they not disappointed me enough, I would have never thought about this. The roots and root causes are very strong.

Every person I have met so far. You all shaped me.

Thanks for always being there for me.

Honest Confession:

I really apologize everyone who bought this book as I'm unable to provide you the out and out end product as I couldn't get this work edited or got it proofread by any professional since it was beyond my financial abilities.

You might encounter a few or may be, more than a few grammatical errors or even blunders and also confusing usage of 'Tenses' here and there because of the lack of editing done by a third party. I tried my best in getting it error-free as I edited it thrice all by myself.

I tried to make it up by making the book interesting (I feel so and I can be completely wrong).

The above confession is no way an excuse for the criticism. I'm open to all the criticism that is going to come. This is my first work and I would really love to hear some honest feedback (criticism is feedback too). Also, please provide me all the corrections that you would like to have, both in terms of grammar and also the story line. Help me in publishing a better work the next time.

Thank you. Let's make the next one a crowd work. Why should stand-up comedians have all the fun?

I

Beach Road, Vizag!

If beginner's luck is true, why does the first love often fail?

For a minute, he wondered who was farther. She or the sky? The sky seemed closer than her, the bride. People may stand close to each other, but substantial invisible distances between them can exist. The ocean is breathing out all the heat it absorbed during the day, and it is only matched by the warmth of all those bright lights set in that Way Above function hall. The moon compromised to be rated second in beauty, allowing the bride to take the first place, at least for that day, for that moment, if not forever. He never thought three knots hold enough power to give him an ultimatum about his life and happiness. At that moment, he could fathom the ocean's depth in front of that function hall. He could hear all those crashing sounds of the waves inside him. The waves hit the shore, his dreams hitting reality. Among all the sounds of those loud drums, he heard a cracking sound coming from somewhere inside. He listened to his heart breaking into pieces.

There is this sharp pain, but he isn't sure where it originated. Either the heart or the brain or from both the places. He isn't sure about anything at that moment. Those few minutes have taught him more than his 24 years of life did thus far. Everything started to hit him simultaneously. He felt more emotions in those few seconds than he has experienced all his life. He lost control over his body. He doesn't know whether he is sitting or standing, alive or dead, dreaming or thinking. He doesn't stand with the reality. He is somewhere beyond the human imagination.

After a few minutes or half an hour, which he wasn't sure, he stepped out to breathe some fresh air. The air inside the hall is intoxicated with the blessings of the elders, who promise him that he will never get her back, which confirms the downfall of his dreams. She got married and he got divorced. She, with someone else and he, with his happiness. He hated himself for giving away the key to his satisfaction to someone else, but then, he questioned himself, was she someone else, wasn't she him? Weren't they one?

He couldn't bear that she wasn't his girl anymore, couldn't see her holding someone else's hand and seeking comfort in his footsteps. He wanted to leave there immediately, so he booked a cab online. The notification on his phone alerted him while he was submerging under the sea of evaporating expectations.

"Mr. Santhosh, the cab has reached your location. Please share the OTP with your chauffeur. Please have a safe ride."

"Vizag – the city of destiny".

He felt he was in a different world, a parallel world where he and his girl were not together and he lived without her. No one ever stressed it enough, but the inability to cry is a big problem. He wanted to let that helplessness out in tears, but he couldn't, probably because he grew up in a middle-class family. Houses of middle-class families aren't big and comfortable enough for someone to cry alone. Someone will catch you crying, and you will need to explain everything. He grew up compressing the tears, and they are taking revenge now. He is all dried up in the eyes; there aren't any tears to come out. The helplessness is growing, and he is helpless about that, too. He realised that one needs to give 100% in everything except for love because you'll be empty when the one you loved with all your heart leaves. There is nothing left for you to look forward to. And the void created by them will be filled with melancholy and sadness.

A

The mobile phone blinked to indicate the notification, and there was a message on the screen which read, "Congratulations, N S Krishnan, bearing the hall ticket number A19100SS011, secured the second rank in the PGCET exam and can choose any course under the social sciences category. Please select your desired subject and attend the document verification program accordingly as mentioned in the website.

"Krishnan read this and couldn't believe that he could be ranked second for his performance. He knew he didn't deserve it for his minimal effort. So, for quite a long time, he wasn't sure about the authenticity of the text message and browsed the official website to confirm the information. But it was the same; he got a second rank. He doesn't even remember when he last appeared for an entrance test; it's been a long time, so he couldn't believe that he was still in the league, competing with the students of this generation.

Immediately after that, he started visiting the university website frequently to be sure of the dates of procedures to follow. Certificate verification, admission process, and hostel details. A web portal was provided for the same. He chose "Journalism and Mass Communication" for his post-graduation and got his certificates ready for verification, for which three days were allocated.

The day has come to appear for the admission procedures, and the summer sun is ready to tease them. However, the giant campus felt pleasant and peaceful. Entering a college campus after a long time felt strange; his earlier degree was from a private college which was quite small in size. This is different; the roads are vast, and the colours are bright, while the rules are, let's not talk about them. He is waiting for his serial number, and as always, he is a bit tensed about these procedures, sceptical about what could go wrong, and just then it happened. Like in every movie and fairy tale, he saw that girl who stood out because of how she spoke and dressed and, more than anything, because of her loud voice. She is shouting at the clerk for something, but that's not what he is concentrating on. He is glued to her face and physique. You don't get to see the beauty of a person's character at first glance; you only get to see the beauty of the body.

She looked like a road in the woods, Like a rose among the weeds, Like a Japanese among Chinese, a need for his deeds and a girl of his dreams.

"Can you stop this, please?" he urged himself. He is focused on his masters and wants to keep himself in check. But then, he noticed that beautiful girls could make you forget about things for a while, if not forever. He is done with the admission and hostel procedures and returns home, while all he can think of on the return journey is her voice and face.

1

A kid was staring at the mirror on the top shelf, which was way out of her reach, and her father picked her up to help her investigate it. The kid is smiling with joy, looking at several reflections of her in the broken pieces of the mirror, which are rearranged with glue, but the breaks are visible, just like the scars on the face of her dad, an Army veteran, whose scars will reach the grave along with him. Startled, Father went to the shopkeeper and asked him why they had the broken mirror in the shop, and the shopkeeper just looked back to the owner, who was sitting in the corner. He smiled and said it was part of his collection and not for sale and so it was placed on the top shelf, out of reach.

Another customer who was listening to this conversation just chipped in

"Doesn't that bring bad luck to the people who look into a broken mirror?"

The Owner replied, "Give it a shot, sir and give me the feedback tomorrow".

He smiled and said, "I would rather keep my luck," and left the shop.

The shopkeeper looks at the owner with a strange look, and the owner understands the question behind it and replies, "We didn't lose a customer; we lost a superstitious customer. My mirrors deserve better people to look at, anyway".

The Shopkeeper looked away from him; he never understood him. He thinks his owner doesn't know how to work out a business, but the shopkeeper never bothered to suggest against it as he is getting paid as promised, irrespective of what the owner earns. For the shopkeeper, that's all that mattered. To earn and feed his family. He never bothered about the mirrors, models, or specifications of any of them, even though he had been working there for more than a decade. There was a time when he tried to advise his owner not to lose customers, but his owner cut him short during the advice and asked him,

"What did I recruit you for?"

The shopkeeper replied gayly, "For the shopkeeper post, sir."

"Oh yeah, for a moment, I thought I recruited you for the post of chief advisory officer."

That was the last time the shopkeeper tried to say something against his owner. Though he thought of advising him after that, he refrained from it in multiple instances. His owner never expressed any of his feelings, anger, disappointment, or disgust. The only way he communicates is through his weird sarcasm. There is even a rumour among the shop employees that their owner suffers a disease that keeps him from smiling. None of the employees saw him smiling, not even at the customers. He is always there before any of them comes and still there even after they leave, except for the lunch and dinner timings. He takes a break of 40 minutes for each, and that's all the time the employees use to make fun of their owner. That happens everywhere, I believe.

II

Three days have passed, and Santhosh doesn't even remember when he reached Pune, his workplace. It's been three days since he last looked at his phone, which now has many missed calls and other notifications. He didn't care about any of those except for the messages from his cricket teammates. A few of those missed calls were from his teammates, and WhatsApp texts asked him to join the team on the coming Saturday. But because he didn't answer and couldn't confirm his availability, his name was dropped off the playing eleven. Nonetheless, he attended the match to watch his team perform. He felt better being there, watching his team play. He realised that if there was one thing, he loved more than her, it was this: Cricket. He returned to his room late in the afternoon and wanted to give his brain a bit of rest, but the body had taken over, and in no time, he fell asleep.

It was past 6 p.m. when he woke up, and some fresh feeling had taken over. His brain is as blank as a newly opened Microsoft Word document. It felt strange to have nothing running in the brain. He got up and wanted to walk and greet nature for a while. A cat crossed his path as soon as he stepped out of the room. He started thinking that this cat might be crossing his way every day, which would have been the reason for all his bad luck. He felt at ease after shifting the blame onto the innocent cat. He felt the weight of the consequences of his actions being taken off his shoulders. It was so relieving that he was smiling unknowingly. He looked around, and everyone was keeping up with the running world. He felt as if he were a tortoise in the human world. He started asking himself,

Did anyone ever blame a tortoise for walking slow? We all accepted that tortoises walk slowly, eat slowly, and move slowly but die late. Why don't we get that few people are like tortoises? We work slow, think slow, act slow, but we love fast. We, by default, expect humans to be in sync with their peers and expect them to work at the same pace and with the same effectiveness. This puts a lot of unwanted pressure and, in turn, makes an individual lose his way in deciding personally or professionally. All these thoughts sounded stupid and irrelative to him as he couldn't do anything to change either the world or himself.

B

Krishnan is a bit concerned about how he would be treated in the college as he would be elder to all his classmates. He finished his degree a few years ago and had a gap before thinking of pursuing a master's course. Now, he would seem like a professor doing a course along with the students. He must figure out a way to mingle with his new peers.

He is already a bachelor's degree holder, but there is always that fresh feeling while you're entering a new class. On his way to the classroom, he is experiencing those strange mixed feelings where he is nervous, excited, anxious, and sceptical, all at once. He moved to the college hostel a day before, and everything looked set until now. It felt strange to carry a bag of books after a long time again; it felt like travelling back in time and being on the first day of his bachelor's degree days.

At his classroom door, he saw that same girl sitting on the first bench and writing some notes. I know what you think: I'm making up a South Indian movie story. But no, similar things do happen in real life, too. The girl you like sits in the same classroom as you do, a pretty girl will occupy the next seat to you on a bus, the flowers do shower when a girl walks off the temple, rainy days do feel romantic, romances do take place between people who are in a relationship. All these things do happen in real life; the only reason why we don't notice them is because there is no background score and no cinematographic elevation for that person. But trust me, they happen; pay attention.

She is in a different costume altogether compared to that day. She is wearing a churidar today and is sitting quietly. Well, these feelings didn't last long. In an hour or so, she is there talking to a guy in a usual manner, which is loud in regular terms. But then, that's how she speaks.

It didn't take long for them to talk to each other and exchange numbers. Fifteen days into the course, they skipped their first class to enjoy a movie, only two of them. He felt that it was moving a little too fast, but then he asked himself, "What is too fast?" things happen in different timelines with different people. With some, you take years to get comfortable; with a few, it is only a matter of minutes.

The next day, he is still sitting in the class, though it is lunchtime, as it would be too crowded in the hostel mess. He was on his phone, reading an answer in Quora, and suddenly, she came and sat on his lap. He is startled. For a minute, he didn't know how to respond; he was just there bewildered. After a few seconds, he brought himself back into the real world and then put his hand around her waist, but with a heart running at a pace that could easily beat Usain Bolt on the field. After that moment, he doesn't notice what else is happening around them. She got up, the afternoon classes happened, she went home, he hit the gym, but none of those things felt like they happened. Time froze for him until she texted him that night.

Prags: what's up?

Krish: You are the one to say.

Prags: Say what?

Krish: Let's talk about what happened in the afternoon.

Prags: Did I make you feel uncomfortable?

Krish: You surprised me.

Prags: You still didn't answer the question.

Krish: No, you didn't make me uncomfortable, but I want to know what prompted you to do so.

Prags: I don't know, I just felt like it, and I did.

Krish: Oh, in that case, I will kiss you tomorrow because that's what I feel every time I see you smiling.

Prags: You can't. You won't

Krish: I will. Do you want to bet on it?

Prags: Let's see.

Krish: I'm warning you; I don't care much about what everyone around thinks. So, be sure before taking on the challenge.

Prags: I don't think you are courageous enough; let's see tomorrow.

After over half an hour of thinking about how to approach the kissing the next day, he asked himself, "What am I doing? Why am I being a teenager again?". Then, he answered himself, the only way to bridge the gaps between generations is by forgetting your age. Along with your age, let go of the ego brought to you by the experiences. Be flexible, be funny and be young. Be a teenager to deal with a teenager; don't be scared to be stupid and crazy.

Her last text disturbed him a little. He wasn't sure why she said that. Does she think he isn't courageous enough to make the move, or is she just trying to instigate him towards the kiss? Anyway, it didn't matter. He would love to kiss her any day, and now, he got a chance; in other words, he got approval from her. All he needs to do now is wait for tomorrow.

2

"One by one carefully", ordered the owner to the workers while unloading the goods. The owner decided to renovate the shop, so all the regular employees have been offered paid leave for a month while he resets everything how he wanted.

"What is there in these packages, boss?" asked one of the guys carrying a very light package on his shoulder but very carefully, as ordered by his boss.

"What do you prefer? An answer to that question or the pay for the day?"

No words were exchanged between anyone post that answer from Acharya, the owner.

It took around 4 hours for four people to unload the whole truck, and there was absolute silence during the entire time. The owner was sitting at one corner, looking at all their work, and was impressed with how they'd taken the orders. Once finished, he called everyone by name and paid them more than promised. That is his way of expressing satisfaction. For some reason, he doesn't like to appreciate anyone through words. That curious guy who wanted to know what's inside the packages received his payment and is waiting at the entry gate. Acharya looked at him, ignored at first, but then, that bloke didn't move an inch and was waiting there, so Acharya called him inside, "Why are you still here?"

"As I'm paid now, I thought I could ask for the answer to my earlier question".

"I've another truck to unload next week. Do you want to be part of it?"

"As long as you pay me".

"Compromise on the answer then, for now."

"Controlling a curious brain for a week isn't easy, but I guess I can manage. See you next week".

Acharya is still sitting in the corner of the room and thinking about arranging the unloaded stock. He has a lot of planning to set the items according to the available space, price range, and people's interests. The life of a person is like a showroom. One must sit and think to arrange the things in order inside their brains to make something out of them and something towards one's life. You can't just have all the items scattered and tell everyone you have them. You must set them straight and let the people see what you're made of, what you're capable of, and what you have to offer.

He sat there designing a blueprint for the arrangement once the stuff reached the shop next week. He is doing them one by one, gradually, starting with finances. He is old enough to fall under the senior citizen category, but no feature of him shows that. Yes, there are wrinkles on his face, and his physical movements slowed down a bit, but he seems way younger than he actually is. His words are still as firm as of a muscular adult's, ears working fine, stubbornness undisturbed from his youth, and his sarcasm intact. By the way, how do we calculate the growth of sarcasm? Do we say that it got better or gotten worse? Maybe, I must say, it has become more effective.

III

Santhosh woke up to an alarm that he didn't set. After sitting up, he realised it was 9 a.m., on a Monday. He wondered which was worse, the day or the time and concluded that the combination of both (9 a.m. and Monday morning) is the worst pair ever, especially for the Employee Species. He habitually listens to motivational speeches every day after waking up. On the YouTube home page, there were inspirational video suggestions. He felt that the algorithm of YouTube understood him better than a lot of people he spent his time with. But then, does he spend enough time with people so that they can understand him? Anyway, he listened to one of those videos which said,

"Irrespective of what it is, get up, dress up and show up That's the only way to achieve something".

That's what he did a few days ago. After she called him, although he sensed something was wrong, he got up, dressed, and showed up, and what happened? Break up. He felt deceived by all these motivational speakers. That was the last time he ever listened to one.

Well, he must show up at the office. So, he got up and dressed up. With eight people on board in that tuk-tuk (A shared auto in west, north, and north-eastern India is called a tuk-tuk) under the highly effective employee of nature, the Sun, in his formal clothing, he is frustrated. The unwanted honks around him aren't helping much. But then asked himself, "Would I be doing the same if I got stuck in the traffic?". He ended up with an answer, "Maybe, " which eased his anger. Humans care about right and wrong only until it comes down to them. When it comes down to their judgment, they find the reasons satisfying.

No sooner had he reached his office than the project manager summoned him. He looked around and saw no cells (they are called IT cells anyway), but it looked like a prison. He eats on time according to the food courts in the office, does whatever his manager asks, sits at one designated place, and gets a number. They call it an identification card with an employee number, but he didn't see much difference between that and the numbers assigned to inmates. Dhiraj, the project manager (generally called a PM in IT terms, and they, most of the time, do feel so), didn't even lift his head to look at him.

"Sit down, please".

Santhosh sat down.

"The bank requires WMS and so you would need to travel to Lagos, Nigeria. Revise and brush up on all the topics concerning WMS and prepare to travel in a week. You will have to perform multiple tasks at the client location. Please finish the pending tasks here and hand them over to any of your peers so that they can work independently without your assistance once you leave. Please ensure you give complete handover; there should be no dependency."

He had mixed feelings about all that went on in the past minute, but above all, there was an important question he needed to ask,

"Dhiraj, what is WMS?"

And now, Dhiraj stared at him and had a moment of silence. Probably, that's the symbol of contempt towards his subordinate for not knowing what WMS is.

"Wealth Management System, a module of our application"

Santhosh returned to his cubicle. He is excited to travel and nervous about his first overseas assignment but is relaxed about one thing: he doesn't need to brush up or revise any of the topics because he doesn't even know what WMS is. He started daydreaming about the foreign lifestyle, the on-site (overseas assignment is called an on-site) salary, and many more perks of travelling. With the onsite in front of his eyes, he forgot about the invisible cage around him and the prison he was considering.

C

During the lunch break, he was waiting in the classroom again. Every one left the class again, and she sat on his lap again. And he is nervous again, unsure whether to take it forward or not. Motivated by many quotes, he wanted to seize the moment and did. He kissed her on the cheek. There are no words after that till the evening, or maybe there were, he doesn't remember. Everything happened as usual again. Afternoon classes happened, she went home, and he hit the gym. When she made a move, his time froze; Even when he made a move, it's again his time that's frozen. He seemed to have lived that moment too much and it gave him so much adrenaline that he was mentally high the whole day. It took him an entire session to come out, and he texted her.

Krish: So, what's up?

Prags: You are the one to say.

Krish: About what happened in the afternoon?

Prags: Do you have anything else to discuss too?

Krish: Did I make you feel uncomfortable?

Prags: You surprised me.

Krish: You are yet to answer the question.

Prags might have giggled on the other end, but he couldn't see it: Do you think girls answer straight?

Krish: Okay, I felt like..... I always feel like kissing you. Today was just the first, in case you have doubts.

Prags: Let's see that too.

Both are getting closer, which is visible to almost everyone in the classroom. Listening to the songs together, eating off the same lunch box, coming and leaving the classroom together, doing all those little things with grace, that's what love offers, grace. When two people are in love, they glow differently. But he didn't want to take any chance of taking it forward. Even though he kissed her and she didn't make any fuss about it, he still didn't want to assume anything to avoid the risk of misunderstanding the bond.

The next day in the class,

"So, are you going home for the festival?" She asked.

"No. It's only three days, and I'll lose more than a day on the journey. I will be here, in the hostel," he answered while reading the *Don Quixote*. If someone stops reading "The Don Quixote" just to answer your question, please understand that you must mean a lot to that person.

"Come home then".

He lifted his head and looked at her, "Are you sure?". If someone takes off their eyes from the book they're reading just to ask you a question, please understand that the question must mean a lot to them.

"Yeah, what's there to be sure, come home. Mom and I will be bored at home anyway."

"Okay, I will come one of those three days. The day when I don't have a cricket match to play".

"Okay, I will confirm whether we're going anywhere or not and will inform you the same".

"But you said you'll not be going anywhere".

"We won't, for long. Grandma's house is nearby, and I will visit them for a few hours."

"Okay then", he sounded normal, but he wasn't. He isn't sure whether she has any feelings for him, but he has developed some, and with those things running in your mind, it's never easy to take these invitations casually. Those cheeky thoughts always run in your mind, probably because we watch many movies where romance starts from these tiny moments.

"It's good that heartbeat isn't loud enough for the people to hear. Otherwise, it would be a disaster. She would have understood that I'm anxious," he told himself.

3

"Damn, these are too heavy for their size", the young man sighed.

"Careful" " shouted the owner from the corner. It took them over 2 hours to unload the truck, but it felt more accessible than it did the last time. They realised it's not tough to work with heavy things, but it's challenging to work with fragile ones. There was even a discussion among the workers the last time they unloaded. One of them said,

"What the heck? He wants us to be careful with every box. I have never been this careful, even with my wife's jewellery". "that's because she doesn't have any." His brother-in-law, who is also part of the unloading crew, replied.

As usual, no one talked while they worked this time. They expected that Acharya would pay them that 'little extra' if they did it quietly, and they were right. Acharya did pay them extra. Money speaks in its ways, loud enough for the observers to listen.

"It's done, and will you tell me what these are, now?"

"Which one? The ones you unloaded last week or the ones you did now?"

"Both"

"The ones from last week are the things which show you what you are, and these fresh ones tell you what you are."

There was evident disappointment from Robin, who was expecting a straight answer from the owner. Now, he must put his brain to work to find a solution to that riddle. He could ask for the solution with a straight face, but that's not something he would ever do. He wanted to crack it by himself. And so, he said,

"I had one question last week and two puzzles now. I'm okay to figure out the answers, but how am I supposed to see you again. Don't say that you've got another load again".

"Well, meet me here once you decode the puzzle. I might have another job for you".

"I hope it's not solving puzzles".

The owner is not listening to him. He is busy moving the freshly unloaded boxes away from each other and settling them into the shelves one by one.

Robin is leaving, and when he is almost at the door, he shouted back, "What are your work hours here? When should I visit to meet you?"

"What?" the owner shouted back, who couldn't hear what the young guy said.

"Give me your timings here".

"It's mentioned on the board outside".

"But there are no timings mentioned on the board; it doesn't have anything on it."

"Oh, I should be available all the time then, except for the obvious meal breaks."

"Big and weightless, small, and heavy. Big and weightless, small and heavy. Things that show me what I am and tell me what I am." Robin left the place, repeating these words, trying to work his head around the puzzles

IV

His friends thought he was waving goodbye, but his hands nervously shook. The organisation provided a cab, a visa, and the headache called an assignment. Travelling abroad has always been one of his dreams, but on the face of it, he is shaking with uncertainty. It isn't always easy to handle what we always wanted because we never think about what happens after we get what we want. The human brain, by nature, is two-faced. It screams, "This is your dream", but then it whispers, "What if your dream is stupid?". People around you hear what it screams, but only you can listen to what it whispers. That's why people generally don't understand each other. We don't always hear what the other people hear in their heads.

After a confusing hour's journey to the airport, he had to worry about something stupid now: the excess luggage restrictions. Just like every other middle-class Indian, he reached the airport way too early, and now, he had way too much time to worry. People often tell you there is no point in worrying; it doesn't solve anything, and so on and on. But being happy doesn't solve anything either. We don't worry because it can solve something; we worry because we have a problem and can't see any immediate solution. All you cool people, please note that worrying, like happiness or sadness, is just an emotional state.

The check-in started, and there it was. The heart was racing like a Rafale jet with no external noise. That's the body's way of responding to uncertainty. It happens to a lot of people when they meet or when they talk to a girl. His turn has come, and it exceeded by 4.2 kgs. There is no uncertainty anymore; he must do something. Yes, it's not much, and he can pay for the excess baggage, but it's enough to panic someone who had never travelled by flight before. He moved out of the line to shift a few items from the check-in luggage to the cabin luggage. He opened his travel bag, which looked like an open South-Indian kitchen on wheels. Biscuits, chips, and a lot of other food items that his team members requested are all present on top. For a moment, he felt as if he was standing there stripped off his clothes, naked. He managed to gather all those pieces of his brain that were roaming here and there inside his head and put them to work. After a few minutes, he moved several items to his cabin luggage (into a HP Laptop bag) which is now weighing over 10 Kilograms. So, guys, if you ever want to know, an HP laptop bag can endure 10 kgs of weight.

After almost a day's journey (with a layover of 14 hours in Dubai), he landed at Murtala Mohammed International Airport, Lagos. Within minutes, he could see the essence of the nation: corruption. Soon after an official called out his name and picked him up from the line. The official paid a few authorities on the way and got Santhosh out of the airport hassle-free. Without him, he would have ended up in the airport for a very long time with no idea about the immigration procedures, this being his first international travel. He was greeted by a guy (in the cargo pants) at the arrival block with a name card. After shaking hands, he said,

"Gedin decor, please."

Santhosh couldn't understand it and said, "Sorry, I didn't get you, come again."

"Gedin décor sir, please."

Santhosh thought to himself, "It's the same thing again. How am I supposed to understand it the second time if it's pronounced the same way?" he said, "Sorry, can you please repeat it?"

This happened a few times, and Santhosh still couldn't understand what he meant. He felt so stupid that he wanted to give that man a chance to punch him in the face. He didn't do that because he knew that man was already pissed and would accept the offer. And it wouldn't sound so good to remember the first thing on his overseas travel is being punched down in the face. He apologised for not understanding their dialect and said,

"Can you please write that down and show it to me?"

The man in the cargo pants opened his phone, opened a notepad file, and wrote that down,

"Get in the car, please."

Santhosh apologised and thanked him. He felt so ashamed that he didn't even look into his eyes after getting into the car. He doesn't remember his face anymore, but he surely remembers his physique because

Santhosh was sure a punch from that big guy would have left him with a distorted face for life.

Nigerian dialect of English isn't very different from Indian English, but their way of using it is new to him. He reached his hotel and his team mates informed him that the client would pay for any of their excess baggage. Another blunt embarrassment right on the face. So, all that effort of shifting luggage, that fast heartbeat, that exhibition of his kitchen in the airport, all for nothing?

D

"You look lean."

Krish is surprised. "But Aunty, you're seeing me for the first time."

She smiled. "I saw you the day you came for the joining procedures. We were in the same line that day. You probably would have only noticed my daughter. I'm old enough to be ignored".

It's a trap, and now, he doesn't know how to counter it.

"It's great you remember me from those few minutes." he tried his level best to evade the trap.

"Oh, that was easy. You were the only one who looked a bit different among the rurally dressed guys there. If I remember correctly, you were the only one who came wearing shoes."

He is taken aback. He never knew that he dressed well enough for someone to notice and remember him from that.

Aunty asked "Coffee?"

"Yeah, Aunty, single spoon sugar." he is happy that the topic is not about him anymore.

"For me too, please", Prags shouted. "She doesn't let me have coffee often".

"Where did you get that voice from? Your mom isn't sounding loud."

"It's my own, it's unique. You don't get to hear that everywhere. Record it, repeat it and cherish it."

"You want me to record it and repeat it? Who signs up for self-torture? I don't".

She tapped on his head.

"Aunty…"

"Shut up, shut up. She'll cut my coffee off."

"Is she troubling you already?" Aunty returned with two cups of coffee.

"Not more than what she does in the college, Aunty."

"What does she do in the college?"

"There is another guy who is as childish as she is, and these two people sit together. That wouldn't have caused me any problem, but then, I sit in between these two, and that makes me the part of every stupid thing they do, and the faculty takes it all on me just because I'm elder to them".

"Ha-ha, he is older than our seniors also", Prags laughed, enjoying her coffee.

"Shut up, finish your coffee and show him the house" Aunty interrupted.

When he heard that statement from Aunty, those romantic thoughts began running in his brain. Guys may never show or admit it, but romance is always in the back of their minds. They went upstairs to see the two individual rooms. In one of those rooms, she is showing him the books on the shelves, but his eyes aren't moving away from her, her smiling face. With each step, he could hear his heartbeat every time she came closer.

"Ok, let's go down now", he urged abruptly.

"Why?"

"It's a good house, just like every other expensive house."

"Shut up, we have a huge balcony".

She doesn't understand him. It's getting tougher for him to restrain himself from kissing her with every passing minute, and them being alone worsens it.

"Nice to know, now let's go down".

"OK", she looked irritated, he noticed it but he could do nothing. The amount of time they spend together is directly proportional to the chances of him jeopardizing their relationship.

"You guys are here already? Okay, go and bring chicken; I'll prepare lunch," Aunty told her.

"Come", Prags dragged him,

"Did you take him along every weekend when you wanted chicken?" Aunty asked, and there was visible sarcasm on her face. Prags left for the chicken without saying another word.

"As you said, there is still that childish innocence in her. That's why we're scared to send her anywhere outside the town for either vacations or education. Her brother is in Pune, the only place I could send her. She never stayed away from me for long except for her hostel days during her eleventh and twelfth. Even then, she used to come home every weekend." Aunty started talking to him as if he were their family member. "She trusts people easily, and because she looks pretty, you know people, don't you? They try to take advantage. Marriage matches are flowing, and it would be easy for me to get her off my shoulders, but I don't want her to get married for the next four years until she reaches adulthood. When I saw you that day in the campus, you looked mature, and I'm glad you are friends with her. Take care of her while at college".

"I looked mature because I'm elder to all of them, Aunty", he smiled, answering.

"That isn't the only thing; how you act and behave says a lot about you."

"Enough of your discussions. Ma, go and cook now," Prags entered.

"She was telling me how you tortured her as a kid."

"Oh, that's all partiality. She likes my brother and complains about me to everyone."

Prags brought the photo albums while her mom was busy cooking. She started explaining the photos, and he was staring at her in all the pictures. She changed over the years, becoming a beautiful girl from an innocent child. It's almost like looking at her growing up.

"So, what did you observe from the photos?" Prags was curious.

"You play guitar", he responded.

"I was expecting more about me than what I do." She is disappointed.

"Something like you were cuter as a kid?" he asked.

"Don't make it up now just because I asked." Disappointment turned into anger.

"No, but It's true that you are just as cute as you were back then."

She smiled but then, with a stern voice, "Enough."

"But tell me, when are you playing guitar for me?" his question is filled with hope, expecting her to do it right there.

"The day when you learn to compliment your girl", she replies.

Before he could say anything,

"I'll rest for a while. I'm used to these naps post-lunch," Aunty said, entering the room.

"Go Sleep; I'll take care of him", Prags responded in her regular loud voice.

"It would be enough if you don't make him run away from here."

They started watching a TV series on her mobile phone. He is so into the episode that he doesn't even realise she is staring at him. She kissed him on the lips; it happened in an instant. He was astonished, and suddenly, many things started to run in his mind, but before any of those thoughts came out, she leaned onto him and kissed him again, harder this time. He joined the act and reciprocated. They kissed for a moment before he pulled out and looked around. She got up, left the door ajar, and made a sign towards him that her mother was asleep. She sat on his lap, leaned towards him, holding his cheeks in her hands, and slipped her lips slowly onto his before interlocking them so tight that time seemed to be trapped between their lips, chained by the warmth of their breaths and stranded by the sounds of their heartbeat. Kisses are temporal moments that introduce you to eternity. Words hold a lot of power, but they often fall short in front of a kiss.

He kisses her passionately while his fingers run over her neck and through to her, and she abruptly pushes him away.

"Leave now," she said, but in a very calm voice.

"I'm sorry, Did I do anything wrong." He feels guilty for something that isn't wrong.

"It's not about you; it's about me; leave now. We'll discuss it later."

He hugged her and said, "Wake aunty up, I'll say goodbye before leaving".

"Why are you leaving so early? We have buses leaving as late as 10 p.m. I expected you to join us for dinner."

"Nope, Aunty, it's okay."

"Go for a movie if you people are bored. Theatres are nearby."

"Movies with him, I won't go. He doesn't even talk in the movies." Prags chirped in.

"When did you watch a movie with him?" Aunty is spot on.

"We all, classmates, have gone to a movie once, and he gets glued to the screen."

"Okay, I'll make tea then. It's 4 o'clock anyway."

He had tea, and Prags walked him to the road from where he boarded a bus. Just when he was about to get onto the bus,

"I love you too," she said and waved at him.

All his doubts vanished when Prags kissed him, and he immediately proposed her. She reacted hastily initially but then expressed her feelings just before he boarded. The window seat in the bus felt even more lovely than it already is. Generally, people slip into their past sitting at a window during a journey. He used to do the same, but now, he is looking towards the future, thinking about the upcoming days and excited about the trip ahead.

#

Robin ran to the shop two days later and started searching for Acharya.

"Boss… Boss…" he began shouting.

Acharya is inside the storeroom reading a book and hears the voices outside.

"Mirrors and Books", Robin shouted. The mirrors were big and light, and the small and heavy ones were the books. 'Things that show what we are' are the mirrors, and 'things that tell us what we are' are the books.

Acharya smiled-the smile that his decade-old employees could never see. Well, Robin doesn't know that, though.

"Do you want to work here?" Acharya asked.

"You mean, working for you?"

"I mean, Working with me."

"What will you pay?"

"Attention to your necessities"

"I guess I'm taking a risk here."

"Welcome to the mini world of books and mirrors."

"Don't we need to have any name for the outlet?"

"We will, once we are ready to have customers."

"How about hiring a few more people to get these things done quicker?"

"Not all understand the importance of handling things slowly. Going slow gives you enough time to think, and that gives you better ways of handling things."

Even without asking his owner what to do, he separated the boxes and moved them to their corners. He looked around and understood which corner belonged to which. Even though there is a doubt at the back of his head about the money he's not going to make by agreeing to work for his owner, he is content with how he has been treated so far and would be happy to have it continued.

"Come here; I will explain to you how we will arrange these things," Acharya called him to his desk, opening the blueprint he drew with a vague idea two nights ago.

After a brief explanation, Robin said, "So, we're going to make this a small maze. The mirrors run through the walls, including every edge and corner, and then, in the middle, we will have books reflected a million times in the mirrors. One has to figure out where it is. Just like it is in the saloons, surrounded by the mirrors."

"Something like that", Acharya replied. "But there is another reason, too. When you have racks, you can't see the books on the other side, but with mirrors on both sides, you get a view of the books on the other side, too. Just a way of making the search easier."

"Yeah, only if they look at the books instead of looking at themselves." Robin smiled. "But I must admit, this is unique. I have no idea whether this is good or bad, but it is new. By the way, what should I call you?"

"Acharya"

"What?"

"Call me Acharya, and Come along."

"Where to?"

"It's lunchtime, and I haven't seen you carrying any lunch boxes."

"Well, I didn't expect to be here so long."

"Expect it from now on."

They walked about 10 minutes across the street to reach a small house with just two rooms and three windows. Robin was expecting his owner to take him to a restaurant and was thinking of all he would order for lunch. Now, his expectations evaporated gradually while climbing the steps in the street. When he entered the house, the expectations were over and out.

"Cut these into small pieces." Acharya handed him a plate and a knife.

"What are you going to make with onions?" Robin asked.

V

It's been three months in Nigeria already, and he has nothing to remember except for three things that happened to him over time. The episodes of the series *FRIENDS, Star Radler* beer (A Nigerian special), and how he was robbed on the road.

After the long working days in the office, he started watching FRIENDS as a refreshment therapy. They used to work from 8 am to 12 pm almost every day except for Sundays. Life is running with numbers—the number of issues raised, the number of problems solved and left pending. There is nothing else to it; it is the same daily. He wished there were other numbers to his days. The number of pages of a book he read, the number of runs he scored playing a cricket match, or the number of places he visited. But that isn't the case. There is no time for that. And so, to overcome his self-pity, he relied on fiction, the romantic comedy of *FRIENDS*, and he never regretted the decision. Every single day when he is low, the show cheered him up. He went to sleep smiling a lot of days, irrespective of the workload; all credit to that show.

His only companion, along with FRIENDS, is the only beer mix in Nigeria made by the master brewer NB plc (Nigerian Breweries), *Star Raddler*. It's a unique mix of the classic Star with the natural citrus juice, and with only 2% alcohol content, *Star Radler* is a natural refresher. At least, he felt so. Spirits are something that lifts your spirit.

The next thing that he would never forget in his life is the way he was robbed. It was a Sunday morning, the only day he was spending with himself. It was a rainy morning (when it rains, it generally rains heavily in Lagos), and he decided to take a walk in the rain. He was missing the monsoons of Pune. The combination of Monsoon and Pune is like a couple on their honeymoon. You experience a lot of emotions and will have a lot of memories to cherish. But that's out of scope here; rains in Lagos don't come with those black clouds or those chilled breezes. They come just the way the water hurries down when the gates of a dam are lifted, complete, adequate, and then stop just like that.

He walked out onto the road to find it deserted. He had been there for over three months but had never thought those busy roads would be so uninhibited. All those things he had heard about Nigeria started creeping in. He was warned about muggings and robberies from the day he told people he would travel to Nigeria. But what he experienced in those three months was nowhere near this. Fifteen minutes into the walk, he was somewhere far from his room, and a guy was coming in the opposite direction. The guy smiled at him. You get that often in Lagos. People respect you for being brown or white here; they treat you and your culture higher. He smiled back, but that fear from the stereotypes was still present. He was about to put both his mobile phones inside and started pacing quicker, but there it was. The guy clicked open a knife, and there were no words, just the movements of his hands. And now, from nowhere, another guy came from behind and was about to grab his mobile phones, but Santhosh resisted by holding the mobile phones tighter, and in a split second, the guy from the back held Santhosh by his waist and lifted him. It all came as a surprise, and before he could realise what was happening, they picked his pocket and left, running from there. They parked a bike nearby, and when Santhosh looked at them, the pillion rider looked back and smiled at him.

The whole thing started and ended with a subtle smile. Santhosh didn't understand what they meant with their smiles, but probably, for the first time, his wallet could put a smile on someone else's face apart from his. He was startled by everything that happened in those few seconds. After realising that he was mugged on the road, he started running in the direction they went to find his wallet, but in vain. He didn't run behind them for the cash or the cards. There was something else. He searched for his wallet for quite some time but returned to his room after failing to find it. Before starting for a walk, he was worried that his wallet would get drenched, but now, he doesn't have to worry about it. Quickly, he deactivated all his bank cards (there was an international card inside). After finishing all those procedures, he sat down and started writing about his experience.

Behind all those papers,

Besides all those cards,

Beyond all that currency,

There was a photograph, her photograph.

It was the only physical memory that stayed.

The photo which shows the faint smile which hides all those fierce scars,

The photo which shows the beautiful face that slams the raw truth on my face,

The photo which has those innocent lips which place the gentlest of the kisses,

The photo which has those tiny ears which distilled all my useless phrases,

And beyond that photograph, there were the memories of 4 splendid years.

That's what you had taken away from me, brother.

But I understand the pain. Your pain of hunger may be more substantial and worse than my pain of losing someone and losing my only physical memory of all my virtual memories. But the pain, in the end, is similar brother.

Note: *This single incident defines neither Lagos nor Nigeria. I have been here for over three months now, and this was the only time that something like this had happened. I walked alone many more times, and there were many smiling faces. Many stories started and ended with a smile but were completely different from this and were very pleasant. Lagos is a beautiful place, and I have a lot of fond memories associated with it.*

After making sure that his experience doesn't stereotype the character of the people of the place, he embarked on time travel, living through all those memories. He constantly pondered why the pillows were mainly made of cotton, and on that day, he understood why. Pillows, more than anything, store your tears, your fears, and all your sorrows. Besides being able to soak in all those emotions, they need to be soft and comforting. Sobbing on a stone doesn't feel right.

E

"Shall we discuss what happened the other day?" Prags questioned him. They sit on a bench in front of the university's central library, their usual discussion spot. That's where they wait every day till her daily commute bus starts, that's the place where they spend most of the time, the area which witnessed their smiles and laughs, the trees which heard a lot of their stories. Probably, nature already knew where it was going to lead. It only talks to you by sending the flowers and breezes, which we often overlook.

"Have you ever been to Daulatabad Fort?" he is looking at the skies.

"Where is it?"

"In Maharashtra, near Aurangabad. It is..."

She interrupted, "Wait, why are you telling me this? Don't divert the topic." She knew he would become a geek when it comes to historical concepts.

"I need to tell you something important. So, please listen to me carefully. The fort has different levels of security to confuse the enemies and trap them inside. It's constructed on a hill which is so smooth that you can't use mountain lizards as climbers. Water filled with crocodiles surrounds the fort and the blind room through which the enemies need to enter because that's the only way to enter. And all this engineering is to secure their king, making sure that their enemies go through all the hardships before they have any chance of reaching to him.

That's what I've been trying to do over the past few years. I was in love with a girl for a long time, and we decided to move on mutually due to several reasons. But it took me a long time to realise that we can only push away a person but can never distance ourselves from the memories, the memories we had with the person, the moments we shared, the days we spent cherishing. After deciding to get separated, I started building a wall around myself, cementing it day by day, year by year, with the bad experiences of mine and everyone I knew. I didn't let anyone reach closer to me, didn't allow any person to understand me or even to know what I felt. Over the years, I just raised the bar. Started the wall, built another layer, and then electrified it. I've done all that because I fear exposing myself and expressing my feelings. I don't say I'd never liked anyone else after losing her; I did, but I didn't tell it because of the fear that someday it has got to end. I wasn't ready to risk myself for anyone. In the last few years, I doubted whether I would love anyone again in my whole life. I locked my heart and threw the key into the bottom of the sea of sorrows so that neither I nor anyone else could enter it. I thought someone would need to break all those walls to even reach me, but then, you've come so simply into my life and without any effort, you just walked past all the barriers I'd constructed within years, and you ran straight into my heart. While I thought someone would need to find the key to open the doors, you have had one". He is still looking at the skies. He believed he wouldn't be able to talk freely had he looked at her, into those immaculate eyes and impeccable face.

"What is the key?" Prags sounded calm, very unlike her.

"That smile, that gentle smile of yours. I never thought someone could easily break me with the simplest of human expressions. Should be your touch as well."

"But how are you sure it's love? It can be just an attraction."

"You know. I sit in the library for most of the day. The other day, when you called me, I was reading a masterpiece from *Fyodor Dostoevsky, "Crime and Punishment,"* which was so interesting, but when I saw your text, I left that mid-way and came out running to see you. I don't ever do that. I never leave my book midway, not for anyone. Reading is a part of my life; it's almost like a part of me. But that day, I left it midway; that's when I realised. I was ready to stop whatever I was doing to see you. That's when I knew it was love and realized I was ready to risk losing myself for you. I didn't even remember leaving the book midway until I visited the library the next day. That's how much I am into you. I generally don't let anyone control my day, but now, you can do that. You can make or break my day with a simple action, sentence, glance, or stare. I don't think that happens with attraction."

"When was that?" she is curious.

"That's the problem: we often don't write down the important dates, especially because we don't know they're special at that moment. Looking back, we remember every tiny detail about that situation, all except for the date."

"You could have mentioned any day because you're in the library every day, and you come out to see me and send me off every day."

"True that, but this particular day stays with me forever. We can't fake the thoughts, can we?"

"Now, don't get into your scientific detailing; as much as I'm proud of you when it comes to your geeky moments, I hate it when you forget me for those slight moments."

"It's your turn now."

"You look good, you study well, you're smart. Even though you are not a tall guy, you aren't short either; I'll compromise on that. You don't always get what you want, do you?"

He is disappointed with her explanation as it lacks understanding of his deeper self. He just said "Okay" in a low voice, losing all that curiosity he had while asking the question.

"You don't know how to take a joke, do you?" she smiled at him.

"I do, but one needs to pick the moments carefully for jokes, is what I feel."

"You treat everyone the same; you respect that fruit-selling lady just as much as our principal. I felt like kissing you the first time when I witnessed you treating her just like one treats their mom, with love, obedience, and gentleness."

"But you have other reasons, too, that I look good. You wouldn't have considered me had I looked ugly, would you?"

"Hemanth wasn't handsome, but I loved him," she said swiftly.

5

"Are we going to have omelettes again?" Robin asked his owner while they were walking for lunch the next day.

"Depends on how well you cut the onions." Acharya responded, "By the way, I decided on a name for our outlet."

"Our outlet?" Robin shouted inside his head, "What is it?" he asked.

"Reflectors and Reflections."

"That sounds good." Robin responded absent-mindedly, as he still works with that 'our outlet' in his head. After a moment, he said, "So, reflectors are the mirrors, and books are the reflections of several people. Good one."

"Either that way or the books being the reflectors reflecting yourself while reading and reflections from the mirrors."

They reached Acharya's home, and Robin was getting ready on the table to cut the onions.

Just when he was about to ask for the knife,

"Wash your face and relax a bit; we will go to the restaurant downstairs," Acharya said.

"Why?" Robin has no idea why he asked that.

"Celebrating the naming ceremony."

"But why did we need to come here then? We could have gone there straight."

"Now and then, a little drama is good for life." Acharya suddenly seems to be a different person. Robin didn't see this side of him in all the days they worked together.

"This is a surprise; I haven't thought about what to eat."

"Don't worry much; that isn't a huge restaurant. You won't have much of a choice there."

Robin tried to start a conversation over their lunch. He wanted to dig deeper into the old man who always shields himself with sarcasm.

"So, how long have you been running this business?"

"Over a decade now."

"Don't you get bored staying at the same place, doing the same thing daily, over and over, with no change at all?"

"I lived my share of uncertainties, and now is the time to stop at a station and rest."

"From your 2-room house, I believe you don't make much business."

"I make enough to meet my necessities, for now."

"So, what did you do before this one? Worked somewhere?"

"So, how long have you been working for the CBI?"

"Ha-ha. Old man, you always escape the important questions. Why? What is so mysterious about you? Do I need to work for CBI to know more about my employer?"

"Nothing so far is mysterious about me, so I am trying to make it now."

The conversation didn't go past that, and they returned to continue their work in the shop. Acharya felt very different while he was with this young man. He is mature beyond his age. Maturity at the right age helps, but before age, it troubles you. You can't enjoy things around you when your maturity levels don't match the people around you.

VI

On a busy day, while Santhosh was busy dealing with the clients, he received a notification that read.

"Dear Customer, Your Account with an Account number ending with XXXXXXX is credited with 151678 INR today".

Numbers are more effective than one thinks. That six-digit figure could bring a smile to his face on that busy day, even if it meant only for a minute or so. He re-read that message over and over quite a few times. Just when he is about to daydream,

"Can you please delete the data from that core table, replace it with the latest data, and re-run the services?" his co-worker urged. In a minute or two, he forgot about the message he received. On that night, after watching *FRIENDS* and before going to sleep, there was a question that bugged him,

"Am I sacrificing the happy life for a comfortable one?"

Had he been in Pune, he would have been playing cricket, which he loves, and reading books, his favourite hobby. He doesn't have time and chance to do those here. Yet he agreed to travel so that he can earn more than what he does in Pune. But is it worth sacrificing the youth for money, for the comforts or luxuries it brings?

Promise someone the future, and they will become your slaves in the present. Time and money together do that often to people. We all trade times of our lives just so that we can live comfortable lives in the future and extend our lives further with the help of medicines to upgrade our "social status" tag. Either we chase money, or the money chases us. Humans seem to have diverted from the paths of happy lives, complicating themselves. We lived this current form of life long enough that we even forgot there was another direction to it. Humans made money once, but now money decides how a human will be.

Exactly two months after the night that thought stuck him, he got his return ticket confirmed. We all leave our homes to fulfil our dreams, but, in the process, unknowingly, visiting home becomes a dream. The paradox of life. He returned to Pune and resumed the office right away. His colleagues noticed a change in his lifestyle. The mobile phone, a new headset, branded clothing, upgraded footwear, almost a new appearance. They pointed that out and were teasing him. He hadn't noticed that himself earlier, but it is true; his appearance did change. Is this what people work hard for? To see those envious eyes around. But he is still the same guy who left for Lagos 5 months ago: inferior, unsuccessful, and imbecile. Probably, this is what money does. It changes you in a way where the world starts noticing you, showing the world a side of you, which isn't wholly accurate. And we all crave that. As much as we call ourselves an intelligent species, we're as strange and clueless as a dog chasing a car.

F

"What?" Krish is shocked to hear that.

"Hemanth was my first love; we broke up a month ago. He is a lean guy who doesn't look good, but I loved him. So, it's not only the looks that I consider."

"You were in love?" he still couldn't understand.

"Weren't you?"

"That's not what I mean, I mean…., I just didn't think of that possibility. I'm neither saying it's wrong nor inappropriate, but I just didn't think about it."

"Okay," she said. His expression and the explanation didn't convince her.

"I have to tell you about many things before we can proceed with this. I'm a very possessive guy. When you're mine, you're only mine. I don't prefer to share the things I like with anyone; imagine how much I would hate to share the attention of my favourite person. I'm not telling you this only because you were in love earlier or to scare you away; it's just a disclaimer I'm putting in front of you before we step further. I don't want you to jump into this and suddenly realise things about me on the way and get surprised at every step of finding yourself in the juxtaposition. I want you to know and understand me as much as possible before making further moves."

"Everyone is possessive about the people they love, so am I. But are you that kind of a person who will doubt?"

"You mean suspecting? I don't. I'll ask everything face-to-face. If I ever have any doubt regarding anything that affects us and our relationship in any manner, I express and explain my concerns over it but will never suspect. And about possessiveness, maybe everyone is, but mine crosses many lines and borders, which it generally shouldn't. Yes, I understand I'm not the only thing in your life, but I should be the most important one. You can have your passions and zeal to pursue whatever you want, and you can love those more than you love me, but there can't be any other person who is more important to you than I am. Your family is an exception, but no one else should be prioritised ahead of me. I hope you understand. I'm not restricting you; everyone has their definition of love, and it should be that way because we're all heterogeneous people and can't love the same way. I'm explaining my way of it. And yes, you will be my only priority; I say that with pride and happiness. It's a pleasure to think about you and only about you. Many of these may sound cinematic, but movies only reflect real lives worldwide."

"Cinematic or not, these are a bit intimidating. Anyway, we just began, let's enjoy the journey, and we can adjust to each other in the process. But I need to admit one thing: you have a great way with the words to put out everything."

"Oh, it's the books. The books I read help me express the things I feel. Often, I think I precisely express my feelings to the point. "

"But, what about my past? Don't you want to listen to that? Don't I need to explain?" Prags is concerned about his pushing-away-the-topic attitude, especially about her past.

"Did you watch the TV series *Sherlock Holmes?*"

"No, but why is that a matter now?" She feels that he is trying to escape from the question.

"Your past is your responsibility, but your future is my privilege. Let's make it pleasant."

She smiled, "so, this sentence is from that TV series?"

"Spot on. But this is the only line I've used from the TV. For the rest of the words, you credited the right person, me."

"Don't you think it's a crime to copy the lines from books and movies written by someone else to express our feelings?"

She sounds and looks childish, but then, out of nowhere, she comes up with a mature question like this. It is often surprising to realise that we never actually know about the other person, even after spending much time together.

"Hello..., come back to the world!" she shouted.

"It isn't a crime. We all share similar feelings. The depth of how much one feels might change, but at the core, it's the same feeling. Not everyone can express themselves in words efficiently, so it's not wrong to borrow words from a poet or an author. We all sing the National Anthem written by someone to express our patriotism, and it isn't treated wrong. Similarly, we can use songs, words, poems, and anything we can hold onto to express our feelings. I perceive copying words to communicate as a lot better than miscommunicating. Moreover, the writer would be happy to see his lines blowing in the wind, helping people to expose their hearts. I don't think there is any bigger reward for a writer than people remembering them or their lines during the most important situations of their lives. It keeps the author alive even after centuries. Feelings live as long as the humans do, words live as long as the feelings do, and a great author is immortal with their work."

"Okay, but I wish to share my past with you, to tell you how we were and much more."

"Then, start with what broke you guys up; start with all the reasons why neither of you could hold on to it, the reasons that you told yourself before you mutually agreed to move on. I don't want or need to know how it ended, but I should know why it ended."

"Okay." She sighed.

"The day you're ready to tell me why it didn't work out, I'm ready to listen to everything that happened between you."

"Okay, I will need more time, I think." She replied and looked away.

6

"But dear, it was an excellent job. It was moving us up the societal ladder; I planned to buy some jewellery your father sold long ago." His mother sounded sad and worried at the same time.

"So, you're worried about the missing jewellery now?" Robin is calm.

"No, that's not what I meant. And anyway, what will I do with it? I will give it away all to my daughter-in-law. So, it's for you people, at the end of the day."

"Don't worry, I will find a girl who doesn't like jewellery."

"Good for you." His mother replied with a formality, but it pinched her inside to think of the possibility of his son not getting her any gold.

For the people who cannot understand what is with the jewellery in the discussion, it is almost a part of the body for Indian women. I guess they feel so different without it on them. It's safe to generalise the statement as it's shared across most of the women of India. If anyone does a survey, Indian women might come on top for the highest gold reserves in the world.

"But why did you have to leave that previous job? Is there anything that you didn't like? As far as I know, it seemed very comfortable." His mom continued.

"That's the problem, it was very comfortable. I was moving into a comfort zone, which makes me incapable of adapting to change if I get used to a comfortable life. Moreover, I want to try something else."

She is utterly disappointed with his answer, but there isn't much she can do. She thinks it would have been different had his father been alive then. He was an alcoholic who always wanted to travel and quickly travelled to the skies. She wants her son to settle well and be recognised by his peers as successful, whatever that means by her standards. But Robin doesn't care about those things; he just does whatever he wants to do.

"What is that other thing you want to do?"

"I'm working for a bookstore."

"What?"

"I am working as a store employee in a bookshop."

"I don't understand Robin. You left your high-paying job to join as a store employee?" his mom is now raising her voice.

"Ma, you won't understand. I want to live different kinds of lives. I want to experience the physical pain of daily labour, the mental stress of a stockbroker, the peaceful mind of a monk, the restlessness of a businessman, a liberal schoolteacher, a strict football team coach, and much more. I want to put myself in their shoes and see life from their point of view, to see the world from a wide range of angles."

"I don't understand why one has to do all that?"

"One doesn't have to do it, but that's the problem; we only do what we must do. Why don't we do what we want to do? I am taking steps towards it."

"Your father did what he wanted to do all the time, and you know where it landed both of us."

"This is not about him, ma, don't drag him into this discussion. He drank all the time to escape his life's reality. On top of that were your tantrums. I agree he was a rogue, but that doesn't need to define how I want to lead my life."

"You too? You, too, blame me for his drinking?" she burst into tears. "He never wanted to take any responsibility, and people blame me for pushing him towards it."

"Stop it, ma, it was over a decade ago. He didn't help while he was alive and is not helping now. There is no point in talking past."

"I'm worried that you might turn irresponsible like your father, which would again lead both of us into all the situations I don't have the strength to handle anymore."

"Ma, pursuing different jobs is not a crime unless they are illegal, and I'm not doing anything illegal. I am just taking risks, which doesn't make me irresponsible, but rather makes me more responsible as I will be accountable for all my actions because I am taking a different route against the odds." He is trying to console her with a logical explanation while her suffering is purely emotional. He continued, "I won't be able to visit home more often anymore, but I promise to try my best to come often." He didn't mean the promise.

****

"Why is it always so difficult for you to answer this question?" Srishti is about to get frustrated. "Why can't you just look me in the eye and tell me whether you love me?"

"Because I don't know. I know it feels great to be with you; you are one of the few people who make me happy, but I don't know whether I would ever be ready for a commitment." He paused and continued, "I am not someone who suits a relationship, and I experiment a lot with life."

"I know you; you want to take risks, and that's okay. I'm just asking you to make me a part of it." she made a point, but it sounded like pleading.

"There is a difference between someone who takes risks in life and someone who risks a life. I hope you understand that."

"I'm okay with whatever you want. I love you enough to bear the problems that come along. I don't dream of a comfortable life."

"That's how it feels now, but in the long run, you would hate me and yourself for choosing this. You won't have the basic amenities of life with me; comforts are not even in the picture. I know how you grew up, all luxuries at your feet, and I won't be able to provide any of that. You deserve better. Let's be good friends just the way we're now."

"Like how we're now? really?"

"Come on, you know what I mean."

She couldn't gather herself to make any further statement. Robin's explanation didn't sound like a statement but an ultimatum. He said she deserves better but it sounded like she doesn't deserve him; she is so typical to have someone like him who is so full of variety.

VII

The routine began after he returned to Pune. He decided to resume everything he missed while he was away. Monday to Thursday nights is reserved for books, Friday night for the movies, and Saturday and Sunday for the cricket. He made some rules and adhered to them very strictly. He returns from the office daily and is hooked to his books until he falls asleep, never uttering a word all the time.

His roommates didn't talk to him, but when they did, they tried to communicate in sign language. They thought that he was dumb(physically) as he never said a word for three weeks straight.

"You are always into your books. Yes, you watched the TV occasionally but never said anything. We all thought you were physically differently abled and didn't know what kind of disability it was. We also couldn't dare ask, so we assumed you could be deaf and dumb. That's why we used signs to communicate. We're sorry."

Santhosh grinned and said, "That's fine; I enjoyed the signs anyway."

"Are you suggesting that we should continue in signs?".

"I would vote in favour of it."

They all chuckled, and one asked again, "But why do you sleep so much? You either read or sleep. I haven't seen you doing anything else, and every weekend, you're nowhere to be seen by any of us."

Santhosh was a little disturbed by the question; it sounded personal to answer about his sleeping time. After a fair amount of silence, he replied,

"I sleep a lot because I love dreams. People are nicer in dreams than in real life. It's our subconscious, after all. And about weekends, you can spot me in one of the cricket grounds around here. If not found there, I would be trekking hills around."

They didn't prolong the discussion further after sensing the indifference in his answers. They, too, would have thought that the days they conversed in signs were better, perhaps.

There are a lot more reasons for him to sleep for long hours. Sleep is a partner we can count on any day. Every time you exhaust yourself crying, sleep comes to your aid. In sleep, you can forget your problems; you don't need to face the real world, and you can dream about the impossible. You can daydream, too, but in your senses, you know that is either impossible or, even if it's possible, you're incapable of it. As Sigmund Freud identified for the first time, we use dreams as a bridge to wish fulfilment. Our subconscious notes everything we want to have but can't. When the subconscious takes control of the brain during our sleep, it projects everything in dreams. In there, we fulfil the wishes that we failed to achieve in reality. How much have humans evolved, for we solve our problems virtually when we can't do that physically?

Apart from sleeping, he only reads during the weekdays, after office hours. Reading opened the vast universe for him. Reading has left him with more questions than it had answered but has shown him a way to think, deduce answers to the questions, and pose new ones. Reading introduces you to the outside world; it takes you to places you could never reach physically, like inside someone's brain who died a hundred years ago. Reading can make you fall in love with someone you've never met, may never meet, and don't even need to. Some people become attractive when you understand their thoughts, irrespective of their appearance. He is finishing a book a week, and in around 11 months, he read over 50 books, most of which are Philosophical. Paulo Coelho, Ayn Rand, Friedrich Nietzsche, Rene Descartes, Sigmund Freud, Dan Brown, and others have significantly impacted him last year.

While he can fill the void inside his brain with the information from the books, the hole inside his heart still longs for her. He misses her way too often, and she isn't there at least to hear that. Emotions are too heavy to carry alone. Over some time, they all stack up and fight against you. We are what we feel. Every time we lose someone, we lose a part of ourselves. A void occupies the places where the person earlier lived, in your head and heart. He understood that he would never be able to fill that space. He and anyone who has lost someone would have a space that will never be filled, and it's not meant to be refilled. We are all incomplete people with missing puzzle pieces. Few of us are lucky enough to find the replacement piece, while others are not. We need to accept it. Anyway, being incomplete doesn't make us any lesser human. Instead, it keeps us honest.

G

"Why is this all of a sudden? You didn't tell me about this before," Prags questioned him sceptically.

"Honestly, I forgot about this until my calendar reminded me yesterday," Krish told her.

"If it's unimportant enough to remember, why don't you cancel it?"

"I planned this a few months ago; I added it to my calendar because I was sure that I may lose track of it at some point because I planned it way earlier."

"So, when will you be back?" she is a bit upset.

"It's a five-day trip, and one day goes for the journey. I will return in a week". Krish is visiting Sri Lanka, which he had planned for several months before joining the college. He forgot about that till he was reminded a day before, which surprised Prags, who had no idea about it. "After the Easter bombings in Sri Lanka, I wanted to know the story from the victims' side and made immediate travel arrangements. But I wanted to visit after things settled down, understand their coping mechanism, and figure out how people return to normalcy. So, I booked my flights for three months from then and completely forgot about that. I didn't plan a fun trip, but I will add a few places now. It doesn't cross the six days; my return flights are also booked. I will do my research, get the story, and will be back. That will help my degree as well, I guess."

"Who wants to visit a terrorist-attacked place?" she asked in her regular voice, categorised as loud for ordinary people.

"Journalists and police. We belong to one of those categories. I don't have the degree yet but seem to have some qualities."

"Whatever, I joined this course just to become a sports journalist or a fashion journalist so that I could get to see and wear various clothes."

"That's some crazy way of appearing towards your goal." he is surprised to see the lack of intention in her towards what she is doing.

"Shut up and come back soon; I will miss you." Prague meant it. Sometimes, you can see it on the faces.

"Had I met you before planning this trip, I might not have planned this. Leaving you for a trip isn't my priority, any day. Anyway, as I said, I will return in a week."

"Don't sound reasonable always; I can't get mad at you when I know you're right."

"I will miss you too, Darling".

Just before boarding the bus, she turned back and said, "Love you", their version of "bye for now".

He smiled and felt complete. "Love you" at the end of the day and looking back at each other while leaving became part of their routine. That simple moment fulfils his day. It's his energy drink till they meet again. He realised why goodbyes are so important and so influential. Even though you'd been years together, it's always the last moment that stays with you for long. Forever, at times.

7

"So, first, you ask for a job, then, you ask for a salary, and now, you ask for a place to live. What next? Should I write off my shop in your name?" Acharya seems to be in a good mood today.

"Let's break them down, one by one.

You asked me if I want to work for you, so it is on you.

When someone works for you, you pay them; one doesn't need to ask for that again.

I'm asking for a place to stay only for a few days.

Writing your shop off on my name, I might say no, but if you think that helps you, please do," Robin smirked.

"Work with me."

"What?"

"You are not working for me; you are working with me. Remember that. That makes a lot of difference."

"Probably that's why he keeps saying 'our outlet'." Robin thought. "Okay," he said.

"Move in today; we will arrange luggage in the evening."

Robin brought in the two bags he left at the door.

"You brought them already; what if I said no?"

"I would have carried them somewhere; it's just two bags."

"Is that all you have?"

"Yeah, a bag of things that hide what I am and a bag of things that tell me what I am." It's time to take a chance at using the code language.

"Clothes and books."

That day, they closed the shop and the renovation works early to make arrangements for his stay at Acharya's place. Robin has been there several times but has never entered any room other than the kitchen. Acharya always made him enter the house from the rear door, which opens directly into the kitchen.

"I will allow you with a single condition. You never enter my room without knocking, and you won't enter it even if it's open when I'm not in there."

"Why would I even care about your room as long as we're not sharing it."

The recklessness of his answer ensured the guarantee that Acharya needed. Robin settled into his room, which is spacious enough for a single guy and with the luggage he has, or that he doesn't have, it's lavish for his needs. He is surprised at how the house is arranged and the calmness of it. There are no chairs, TV, fridge, or anything fancy. Walls are as plain and as faded blue as a sky after rain. After looking at his room, Robin realised that the kitchen was the densest, with only a stove and a few necessities.

His room only has a little wall wardrobe to keep his clothes and books. There isn't a single piece of furniture in the house except for the two bean bags.

"You sold all the stuff for drugs?" Robin seems to have gone too far ahead there. For a moment, he forgot that he was talking to someone almost thrice his age.

"I sold them individually each month, realising I didn't need them. I don't need drugs; I'm always high." Acharya is busy with something in his room. Robin, who was tensed for a moment after involving drugs in his statement, is relieved now as Acharya didn't take it to heart.

After they settled down with the deals of cooking schedules and stuff, both went upstairs onto the terrace. They sat there for a long time without saying any words to each other. Finally, Robin said,

"I like it dark. I will sit here for a while. I also wanted to say, you may leave whenever you want, but it would feel awkward to give the old man permission at his own house."

Acharya smiled, "where did you work before?"

"Banking sector, why?"

"Just wondered, looking at you talking to one of our customers today. You were persuading them with a determined approach, which explains the background experience. But may I know the reason behind the shift of jobs?"

"I was a technical guy at a bank. I had nothing to do with the customers. This is my first direct experience with customers. That's the reason behind the shift of jobs, to see another side of the coin, of every coin. Jumping into a sea of uncertainties gives me chills, and I like it. Before the bank, I was with construction for a few days, where it was just physical labour, completely different from my bank job, where I didn't move my body an inch. Now, I am with you, interacting with people, a completely new area again, and I'm glad I'm doing it well."

"So, you've seen a fair share of comforts while working in the banking then. Where did you stay while working construction?"

"With the group."

"How did it feel to have lost all the comforts and come down to sleeping on the bricks you lay?"

"It felt new, it felt different, but I guarantee you it didn't feel difficult because, for one thing, I wasn't pushed into doing this. That was my conscious choice, and I liked doing it."

"Good for you. Ever been in love?"

"What, boss, are you trying to get inside my head? I am telling you I spend a lot of time there. It's too crowded, chaotic, and not a great place to be."

VIII

After almost a year of submerging in books and movies, Santhosh got another assignment to travel again. This time, to a beautiful island nation, Mauritius. He knew he would be paid less than the previous trip, almost half of what he was offered earlier, but this destination is always in the top 10 of his travel bucket list. And how better can it get when you visit it at the expense of the organisation you're working for? But the experiences of his earlier assignment still haunt him. He had no time to read, travel around, and no time for cricket. So, he ensured that his Visa and appointment lasted only three months. Sacrificing three months of hobbies to travel to one of his dream destinations sounded balanced enough, so he said yes to the responsibility.

Three days before the journey, he began googling for all the places to visit, food to try, beverages to drink, and trying to understand the local traditions. He made an extensive list of places to cover, unlike last time, where all the places he covered were the workplace and the back seat of a car he used to commute to that workplace. He figured out that the work-life balance in Mauritius is so good. People don't stay at their desks after 5 p.m. in the evenings; weekends are actual weekends. Besides, there is one clear advantage this time: he knows that the client pays for the excess baggage. He was the first to travel from the team, and two more seniors will meet him at the client-provided accommodation.

He was in the line for the check-in procedure at the same airport again, Mumbai. Standing in the bar, all he could hear was indistinct whisperings, that rustling sound of the bangles, and giggling voices. For a minute, he stepped out of the line to see what was happening and understood that he was the only single guy in that line. Everyone else seemed to be on their honeymoon. He knew Mauritius was a famous tourist location but didn't expect all tourists to follow the honeymoon code. Standing in a line and realising that everyone else is going to party and have sex and you're just going to sit in front of a laptop is depressing. He opened his notes and wrote them down,

"Never go Mauritius alone, especially if you're single".

He seems to be the ambassador of the embarrassing airport experiences.

After the check-in procedure, he didn't reach the departure gate till the final call to avoid all those happy couples standing hand-in-hand in the boarding line. He doesn't understand why people rush to jump in; standing in bars doesn't upgrade their economy seats to business class. He never understood what kind of satisfaction that gives. They are just going to sit in another chair again. If that's not the pilot's chair or any chair in the cockpit, why hurry? Why not wait and go when your time starts?

It is a seven-hour flight to Mauritius from Mumbai (via Seychelles; Seychelles is another beautiful island nation). He is the first from his team to be there; the other two would reach there by that night. The client informs them that they will be picked up at 7:45 a.m. and dropped back at their places by 6 p.m. every day except for weekends, and they will need to pack their lunch by themselves. So, technically, his school days will be back.

It's a new, stressful and responsible ask for him to handle the clients independently. He is the first to represent his organisation there, which makes him accountable for the standards that will be set. Everyone preceding him will be evaluated depending on his performance. He understood those invisible and untold responsibilities that added to the pressure. He is set to sit with the client's IT team. The other two members of his team represent the functional team (they educate the client about the product), while he is the one who provides technical support. The available team changes every 15-21 days, but he will stay there for 90 days.

People in technical rooms are like inactive volcanoes with lava burning inside but look so cool to the people outside. The air conditioners in the rooms help, too. That's how the software employees are. People who look from the outside only see the beauty of appearances, while internally, they're all burnt up. When he entered the room, he noticed a girl sitting across his chair. She is so hot that he wondered whether the air conditioners in that room are placed to nullify her effect on the people. For a moment, his responsibilities, work, pressure, and everything are burnt in those flames of her beauty. He is surprised how something hot can cool you off. At that moment, he understood what smokers would probably feel while taking a puff; the cigarette cools your tension off while it is losing itself. It took him a while to come back to reality. He had loads of technical work to do, but he was sitting there admiring the artwork of God. Being the only foreigner in that room, he attracted some attention, both unwanted and wanted.

H

"Sir, just come out of the gate, and you'll find me at the end of the road." Manjula, the chauffeur, talked to Krish over the phone.

"Sure, I will be there in 5 minutes." he disconnected the call over WhatsApp and got immersed in collecting his luggage from the belt. After that brisk checking at the exit gate, he stepped on the Lankan land, the teardrop nation. Now, he had to look out for his chauffeur, who mentioned that he would be waiting at the end of the road. Now, the question is, which end? He came out of the exit gate, and there was a queue of cars waiting outside, and Krish wasn't sure which end to go to. He just started with one end as there was nothing he could do.

"Hi, are you……" Krish didn't even ask for the chauffeur's name in the call. "My chauffeur"

"I would be anyone's sir", reply came as quick.

"No, are you waiting for someone named 'Krish"?

"I surely will if he pays."

Krish is frustrated but realised that that wasn't the end he was looking for, there was a moment of relief too as that conversation ended. He went to the other end and saw a man standing at the car's rear end, trying to call someone.

"Are you here to pick Krish?"

"Mr. Krishnan?"

"Thank you, finally. You should have told me which end to come in the call."

"Sir, I've been trying to call you for a while now but have been unable to reach you on your mobile."

"The earlier call was a WhatsApp call, Mr…"

"Manjula, Sir!"

"Yeah, Mr. Manjula, the earlier call was over WhatsApp, and that ran with the WIFI provided in the airport. I forgot it was a WhatsApp call in the excitement of stepping into Sri Lanka. Only after coming out had I realised that I didn't have any means of contacting you as I didn't have the SIM card with the local network yet."

"Oh, Sir. I forgot. I'm supposed to hand you one. The Agency has instructed me to give you a sim." He opened a pouch from the back seat of his car and handed it to him. "This one comes with the best network here, sir. You can use it as long as you stay here. It's been charged with an unlimited complimentary package from the Agency."

"That makes it so better. I've been wondering and a bit worried about it. In these odd hours of the day, I would have got nowhere to get a SIM card."

"Yes, Sir, these early morning flights are so uncomfortable in all possible ways."

"Yeah, for both of us," Krish smiled. After a few minutes of talk with Manjula, Krish was getting sleepy and asked him to stop the car to move into the rear seat so that he could sleep peacefully without affecting the chauffeur. He jumped into the back seat, and just when he was about to fall asleep, he started wondering why luck always plays spoilsport in his life. Why didn't he find Manjula on the first attempt, at the end of the road he first walked? Why is the correct switch always the last one on the board? Why is the room that we always need to go to is on the floor which has no elevator? Why is it always our flight that gets delayed? Someone who invented the English language must be a fascinating and intelligent person. Luck and suck are words that are just a letter apart from each other and are as close as they appear. Luck does suck more often than not.

He woke up to the sounds of the birds and was in a semi-sleepy state, wondering whether he was somewhere in the middle of a garden, but to his surprise, he was in front of his room, the room allocated to him in the resort. Pleasant surroundings started his morning so well.

"I will wait here, sir, fresh up and come back. We will visit Sigiriya and the elephant orphanage today." Manjula brings Krish back to the real world while he is still mesmerised by the resort's beauty. "Or if you want to take rest for some more time…."

Krish interrupted him, "No, the nap in the car suffices. I will be back shortly."

They stopped for breakfast, where a small outlet, painted in shades of yellow, attracting many visitors. Krish inquired about the local food he loves, similar to the Kerala dishes. He had a light breakfast, but it was all healthy grains and vegetables. He went up to pay the bill and said,

"You are all women here; nice to see so many independent women," Krish told one of the outlet's employees. The lady smiled.

"Sir, it's an all-women outlet; we have several of these kind of outlets all-around Sri Lanka." Manjula chipped.

Sri Lanka has been surprising him at every step so far. The tranquillity of his resort, then the all-women resto and now, the bill, which is so casual for such good food.

"Add his bill to mine," Krish told the lady.

"But he cleared off his bills, sir" She replied.

"Our organisation doesn't let our clients pay for anything they're not supposed to, sir." Manjula smiled with pride.

"Must be an honour working for such an organisation."

8

"We don't sell them here, sir. We don't have a religious section in our shop. If we bring those books, we will be forced to place them in the fiction section, which many of you wouldn't like." Acharya answered one of his customers who was searching for a religious scripture. He wondered why a customer had gone to him while Robin was in charge. He moves out of his corner chair to check on him, and Robin is seen outside the shop answering a call in a very animated manner. He seemed to be all frustrated with how he is throwing away his arms. Acharya stood at the door, observing him for a few minutes before entering. He didn't want to be like all those old people who poked their noses in other people's businesses.

Robin didn't seem comfortable the whole day in the shop. He used to sit in a corner and read the entire day when there were no customers, but today was different. He was pacing all over the sections, cleaning the books that are already clean, and just keeping them all in a particular order. He did all those subconsciously. Acharya observed the whole day, and there were moments when Robin caught him watching, but he didn't care; he was mentally elsewhere.

Acharya asked Robin to meet him on the terrace that day; their terrace meetings are helping both of them. After dinner, Robin is the first to reach the deck as Acharya cleaned the utensils. Their schedule has his name on it today.

"I'm sorry, boss, I should take the job of cleaning the utensils every day. I should consider your age from now on." Robin's words felt very sincere.

"There is a reason why I like you better than everyone else in the shop; you never made me realise I'm old. From the first day, you talked to me like you do to your contemporaries. Continue it."

Robin liked it, but something kept bugging him at a corner of his heart to see the old man hustling.

"Weren't you married?" Robin asked the old man, staring at the pond beyond their building, glued to the reflection of the moonlight.

"No, this is your time to answer. I saw you were worried over the call in the morning. Can we discuss that?" Acharya is concerned.

"I admit that I like her and her presence around me. She keeps me happy, but I don't like the responsibilities. She loves me, and I know it, but I can't take it a step further. Though I told her I couldn't have her in my life, I wanted to. My brain and heart hate each other, I guess."

"No one likes responsibilities, Robin; otherwise, Monday mornings wouldn't have been this sad. In fact, the modern way of measuring success involves the number of happy Monday mornings. We all want lives of freedom, but the beauty lies in balancing them. Every one of us hates one or another kind of responsibility. Some don't like taking care of elders, some don't like having kids, some don't like working, and some don't like all of these, but if you're of that kind, you wouldn't have been here exploring different forms of life."

"That's it; I don't like the responsibilities of a commitment, then."

"But did you ever try it? I believe you read a great deal from the sack of books you carried with you. I guess it's a lot of philosophy, too. But you can't judge the world by just the books you read, written hundreds of years ago. Live them, understand what they mentioned and see whether that applies to you, too. They may still hold, but it was the perspective of that particular person. Why don't you try and make your version of it?"

"But won't I become one of them if I live the same?"

"What are you scared of, Robin? Are you scared of living like them, or do you fear living like them because that makes you another commoner who wouldn't be recognised by the world any differently? Because even if you live a different life, the world might not care. More importantly, why would you become one of them? You are your decisions. If your thoughts are different from everyone else's, you will surely live a different life."

"But isn't that a risk?" Robin's brain and heart are commuting between the stations of confusion and acceptance.

"Aren't you the one who enjoys the sea of uncertainties? And why are you worried about risk because it is so hard that it might break your heart one day?"

"Hmm." Robin is quiet, and the darkness seems to have swallowed him into the depths of silence. Acharya kept quiet for quite some time, giving Robin the time to sink it all in.

Robin, Acharya, and their two mutual friends, silence and darkness, had a meeting on the terrace that night.

IX

There they are, the happy hours, the Friday evening. Talk to any IT employee; they will explain the precious times of their lives, most of which are Fridays. Just imagine how vital Fridays are for almost everyone. Every new movie release, happy hour in the bars, and stand-up shows in the houses, all of them start on Fridays. Friday evenings are the gateway to paradise, the path to freedom, the entrance gate to the trance of the weekend. Santhosh prepared a list of places to visit the next day and made arrangements accordingly. The other two colleagues agreed to join him as well. They made a deal with the same transport guy who helps them commute daily to the office.

They began their first-weekend tour with the Shiva temple in Grand Bassin, a holy temple in the heart of the nation. It is a sacred place for Hindus and is visited by nearly every Mauritius tourist. They visited several beaches before returning home, and he couldn't enjoy any of them. This weekend experience seemed like the extension of his airport experience, with all the beaches filled with the newlyweds or the people in love. He couldn't be himself because of the abundance of love around him or maybe because of the lack of love for him. He walked along the coast alone (his colleagues started video calling their homes) and finally met a guy who wasn't with his girlfriend, who was playing with his Drone. Santhosh sat with him and fell in love with drones. If he ever bought one, he would dedicate it to all the couples on that beach that day.

The average temperature of Mauritius varies between 20 and 27, which is very cruel. For a deep-hearted Indian, that's an ideal temperature to stir up memories. Earthquakes, tsunamis, and floods are natural calamities that can turn our lives upside down, but we underestimate the cruelty of beautiful nature. Pleasant Moonlight, cold breezes, and tranquil beaches can turn us upside down, too. We never know how many people are suffering parallel to us, somewhere in the world, unable to sleep, think, and move on. Somewhere, the same full moon might be pushing someone into the deepest thoughts of depression just like it's pushing you. For all those who are deep-hearted, who love with no bounds, who suffer without boundaries, who are experiencing melancholy all around the world, brothers and sisters, we're not alone. There are thousands of us. Hang in there; we will fight through; we can stand this storm, any storm for that matter. But once you withstand it, let the world know your story; let us all learn from it.

After finishing their dinner, Santhosh walked out to his balcony with a coffee in hand, and the brain was ready to press the knob, "Time to fuck-up". Several knobs are in close availability to the brain; few of them are

"Time to panic."

"Time to jump to conclusions"

"Time to be offended"

But activating any of these means activating the "Time to fuck-up" mode. This time, it's different, though. Just because the brain is so free to roam around in the wilderness of the vast universe, it wants to fuck up the timeline of his life and bring in all random stuff to relate with each other. Returning to your conscious self isn't easy once you submit yourself to a particular feeling.

That quiet night,

Those dark clouds and chilled breezes,

A faint drizzle,

Dancing trees,

The cold floor under his feet,

Dimly lit horizon,

Everything was reminding him of her. It is just the first week of his stay here; he must weather that storm for at least three months. Mauritius is a dream destination for couples and singles; it's a destination that leaves them in dreams.

I

"Flight is delayed by 1 hour and 40 minutes. I'm sorry for the inconvenience. Please be at the airport 3 hours before your journey," the message on his phone read.

"As expected," grunted Krish.

"Is the flight delayed, sir?" asked Manjula.

"How did you know?"

"Sir, you're not the first one I'm dropping at the airport." Manjula smiled. "Shall I drop you at any restaurant nearby so that you can have your dinner before reaching the airport?"

"Nah, that's fine. Drop me at the airport. It would be getting late for you."

Five days in Sri Lanka passed relatively quickly, and he covered all the places that he made a note of. They are returning to the airport to catch his return flight.

"Spend some quality time with the kids." Krish tipped him. "Thanks for the cooperation and all your crazy stories. It's been a pleasure spending the past few days with you."

"Thank you, sir. You got my contact information. You know whom to call the next time you're in Lanka," Manjula drove away smiling.

Now that he had more than 4 hours to spend at the airport, Krish started to roam around to find anything interesting, either a person or a scene or anything. He came across a man carrying his kayak bargaining at a coffee shot who looked French, a Sri Lankan lady running around behind her toddler, an old Indian man talking to his granddaughter over a video call, and an African lady reading some business-oriented book.

An hour later, after checking in his luggage, Krish moved to the prescribed gate, sat there, and started reminiscing about his trip. He was awestruck by many things during the last few days. Sri Lankan food habits, their helping nature, punctuality, hospitality, honesty, discipline, and a lot more. After re-living those experiences inside his head, he took his laptop out of its hibernation and started penning down his project report.

The Project Report:

A Tear Drop

Often referred to as the Tear Drop in the Indian Ocean, Ceylon (the earlier name of Sri Lanka) is one of the world's most beautiful and serene island nations. The most fascinating thing about Sri Lanka is the surprise to the size ratio that the nation offers. A country with an area of less than 26000 square miles, which is almost ten times smaller than Texas, has a lot to offer to its visitors. For a traveller, every other destination is just a drive away. With a proper plan, you can be amazed at the fantastic maintenance of a historic place, and with a drive of four hours, you'll reach a chilly hill station and yet another four hours and there you go, leaning back in a comfy chair facing the fierce waves crashing right beneath your feet.

The well-preserved ancient hilltop palace Sigiriya, the southern beach city Galle, hill station Nuwara Eliya, often called Little England, home for the famous Sita (Character from the Epic Ramayana) temple, Dambulla Golden Temple, ancient city Anuradhapura, the gem trade centre Rathnapura and if we start listing, there are a lot more places for a tourist to concentrate. Above all, one will be amazed by the Pinna Wala Orphanage. It is an orphanage that started with just five babies, and now, it's the largest herd of captive elephants in the world. Did I forget to tell you it's an elephant orphanage? Sri Lanka has an elephant orphanage, home to over 90 elephants, with 48 mahouts caring for them. Elephants showering near the Maha Oya River is an incredible sight to watch.

And then, the people. It isn't an exaggeration to say that Sri Lankans are the most generous I've ever met. It's not only about the way they treat tourists but also about how they treat themselves. Look at each other with respect, and everyone seems to take care of their health. Their eating habits are just excellent.

The Tear Drop in tears

With diverse landscapes, Sri Lanka is a tourism-dominated nation that has been peaceful post-LTTE reign, which ended in 2009. The government planned to become the best tourist-attracting nation (measured by the number of tourists per year) by 2020, but a shocker in 2019 changed many things. The lives of thousands of Sri Lankans have turned upside down overnight directly; and indirectly, the numbers amount to millions.

21st April 2019, Easter Sunday, the day when Jesus came back to life, defying death, and on the same day, many of his devotees reached him, unable to defeat death. Three churches in Sri Lanka and three luxury hotels in Colombo (the commercial capital) were targeted in a series of suicide bombings, resulting in 267 casualties, with 45 foreign nationals at the least and over 500 injured—two extremist thoughts and over 267 dead bodies and thousands of departed souls.

Three months into the attacks, the world forgets as it runs at its own pace, but many Lankans' lives came to a standstill. The impact of such an attack will have a significant mark on this Buddhist-majority Island, which not only lasts for months or years but decades. The episode almost nullified the tourism that Sri Lanka promoted over many years. There were no tourists, and the restaurants, hotels, tourist operators, guides, and chauffeurs ended up with no work. Unemployment made its way to the centre.

"I sat for over two months at home without anything to do, sir. No calls from our organisation or anyone else, and I could ask for nothing. Different ethnicities have always graced us in every part of the country throughout the year, and I couldn't see a new face around me even now, three months after the incident. Thanks a lot for visiting us at this time. This means a lot." Manjula turned emotional, explaining the crisis.

Kandy (a city far from the attacks that had happened) is hit with the same intensity. The businesses around the town are dented significantly.

"Sir, you get these gems for half rate now because of the fallen business rate due to, you know, the incident that took place a few months earlier. Thanks a lot for helping us rebuild the world's faith in our hospitality, " a gem store manager said.

And there had been petty communal riots in several parts of the nation for months after the incident. Though it can all be reported as the failure of Sri Lankan National security, talking about roots, the chaos was just the result of someone's extreme love towards their religion.

Had the extremists ever asked themselves whether this was all worth it? Is love for anything ever supposed to result in ending lives? Can war ever bring peace? Few people failed to ask themselves fundamental questions, bringing tears to the Tear Drop.

After jolting down his experiences, he felt more attached to the place, the serenity, and its people. Probably that's how it's with the love, too; we get hooked more to it after bringing it out.

"Boarding for the flight with the number so and so that reaches Chennai is about to start in a few minutes. All the passengers are requested to reach the gate number xxx".

9

"What are you thinking about Robin?" Acharya asked him, who was staring at the moon quietly.

"I am just remembering the moon references in the poems. I wonder which is true: are all beautiful things made feminine because most ancient poets are men, or is it the other way around that only men turned into poets because all the beautiful things are feminine?"

"That must be one heck of a topic for research; it includes history and literature. Why don't you try it, Robin?"

"According to Hindu mythology, the moon and Earth are masculine. So, even in there, the men revolve around the women. Isn't that stereotypic Acharya?"

"That's one way to look at it, but Earth is considered a supreme power. So, the moon must be revolving around only as a devotee."

"Acharya, do you know that Jupiter has 79 moons? Did you ever wonder what would have happened had Earth had 79 moons?"

"Humans are balancing that missing number of moons with artificial moons (satellites), anyway."

"No, what would all these poets do? What will they compare the beautiful faces with? What would be their reference for immaculate girls?"

"Oh, there can be a lot more. Poets are capable of using anything."

"Like what?" Robin is curious.

"As beautiful as a lotus petal,

as reflective/shining as a mirror made of metal,

as soft as a rose,

as plain as prose."

"I haven't read these anywhere, Acharya."

"Not everything is written, Robin; you must listen to people. And let me tell you one more thing: you might have read many books describing how a full moon brings beauty to the sky, but I know someone who said that night brings beauty to the moon because you would never notice a moon in the light. He went to the extreme to say that the moon owes its beauty to the nights."

"The more you think, the more it makes sense, he said. There is something so extraordinary about the darkness. And this guy, you know, did he hate the light?"

"I asked him the same thing. But he said, 'Embrace the dark, enjoy the light.'"

"Acharya, why do you think so many people fear the dark?"

"The burden of truth is so much that we all are comfortable living the lives of lies. Due to all these years of fake layering, most of us must dig deep to recollect what we are. We try to understand the people around us, but one can never fathom the depths of ourselves, let alone the others. We think we fear heights, but we fear depths, be it the people or places. We are scared to even look that deep, afraid we might look at our abyss. I'm not talking about the lies we tell or our mistakes but about the core of what we are. It's astonishing how people evolve every day, but deep down, they never change a bit. And that is why darkness is dangerous; it opens the inward doors. It forces people to introspect, and as I said, we're scared to look at our deeper selves."

"That's profound, professor. But why do you and I like the same darkness?"

"Because we like to suffer. Suffering fills all those gaps in our hearts, giving us that feeling of completeness."

Robin is left speechless. He is surprised at Acharya for his deep understanding of themselves. It is almost like he is reading off Robin's file.

"Why did you assume that I like suffering?"

"I don't assume, I deduce, but I might be wrong. You like to sit quietly and think. Yes, thinking solves many problems, gives one a chance to predict the outcomes, and helps with precautions, but all that has a cost: going through the pain of those situations in your head instead of in real life. To figure out a solution, one needs to eradicate the chances of failure; one needs to think of all of them and live them in the head. Though thinking is regarded as the highest form of human ability, the other end of thinking is misery and distress. And I also know that you like silence. Silence is so nerve-wrecking. We often mistake it for peace. For the outsiders, it's peace; for those who feel it, it's the war inside your head. Battles we face in daily life are nothing compared to the battles we fight inside our heads. We are prisoners of our thoughts. We like to believe that we control our thoughts, but they control us, and we follow orders. As Arthur Schopenhauer said, A man can do what he will but cannot will as he will."

X

Two months have passed, and four different sets of functional team members came and left in those 60 days. Santhosh became an unofficial tour guide for them now, being there for two months and nearly covering all the places. Though he is the youngest of them all in terms of age, he's the oldest in terms of experience in Mau.

Another weekend had come, and he received a phone call from an unknown number.

"I'm sorry I've taken your number from one of your teammates; I hope you don't mind."

"Well, I need to know who this is to decide whether to mind or not."

(Giggling) "Sorry, it's me, the girl you've been smiling at for two months and never talked to."

"Sarah?"

"How did you get to know my name?"

"I'm sorry that I've figured out your name from your teammates; I hope you don't mind."

"Well played. Tell me, are you free tomorrow?"

"Depends on what you have to offer." He smiled.

"Let's go on a small road trip to the North. Are you…"?

"I'm free." He responded before she could finish the question.

Minutes after the call ended, he wondered, is this true? a foreign girl had asked him to go on a date. That's a strange feeling for a South Indian to be called on an official date. South Indian youth go on many dates without realising it. But knowing it upfront made him a bit nervous. Though he wasn't expecting anything from it, he felt excited to go on a date with the hottest girl in the group. He accepted that what's been shown in the movies is not too far from reality and that good things do happen to ordinary people, too.

The sun is bright, yet the temperature is within the 20s, ideal for a date. The breakfast in the morning tasted better than a lot of days. Paulo Coelho was right; when you're good and happy internally, things around you feel good, too. He knew she would pick him up, so he is waiting at his place, looking out the window at the blue sky.

An hour later, his phone buzzed, and she left him a message which read,

"Please come down; I'm at the parking area."

He forgot his software etiquitte for a moment and didn't care to respond to the message. If you're wondering what software nature is, it's the responsibility of an IT engineer to respond to a text or a mail irrespective of the position they are in; even if you're about to die, your superior expects a reply, probably, something like,

"I'm hanging off a cliff; give me a minute to check the mail on priority and think of my life on a second priority".

He got to the car, and she was surprised to see him in his shorts and a Tee.

"Is this how you go on a date?"

"I have never gone on a date before; this is my first."

"Oh, come on; you don't need to lie to flatter me."

"This will be awkward; you don't trust me when I say I haven't been on a date. Once I return to India, and if I tell them that I went on a date with you, they won't trust me either," he replied with a straight face, with no smile or expression.

She drove all the way up North end of the Mauritius. Well, all the way, which is around 170-200 km. Mau is a tiny nation whose longest road wouldn't cross 200 km at any part of the nation. He noticed there were only sugarcane fields all the way; no other crop was seen along the road. He asked her,

"Is Sugarcane the major crop here?"

"Sugarcane is the only crop here. It's cultivated in more than 80% of the arable land in Mauritius."

"Exporting everything?"

"Besides exporting a lot to the European Union, consumption is high too."

"No wonder you people are so sweet."

She looked at him in some way that he couldn't understand. Well, that's how it is with guys. They don't even understand when you talk, and the girls expect them to appreciate their looks and subtle expressions. Dear girls, if you want guys to understand, spit it on their faces. They either wipe that away or deal with it, but it's useless if you give them clues. Neither you nor they get anything from those clues except for the misunderstandings. Clues and hints don't mean anything to the guys. It's a strange coincidence that many poets who write about feelings and emotions are male, and those who don't understand them belong to the same group. But it is what it is, and we need to accept it. He wanted to know what she meant by that look but decided against it, thinking that he might not understand even after she explained, which would make him look dumb.

By the time he woke up, they were somewhere parked at the beach. He slept off on his date, sitting beside her in the car. Welcome to the South Indian way of dealing with girls. He woke up to the crashing sounds of the waves on the shore. She is sitting on a bench a few feet away from the car, looking at the sea. He walked up to her,

"I'm sorry; how long have we been here?"

"Who is that girl?"

He looked around and said, "Who?"

"Who is that girl whom you miss?"

"Hey, nothing of that sort; I just didn't sleep enough last night, and your roads were so smooth that they threw me into the hands of the slumber-goddess."

"You haven't looked at me for most of the drive; you were looking at the window, the roads, the passing trees, keeping quiet all the time. I could sense it; you are missing someone. That can also be your family, but I strongly feel it's a girl."

"She is married." he wanted to lift some thoughts off his head, which had been too heavy to carry.

"So, do you want to talk about it?"

"Some other time, maybe."

"So, tell me, what do you love to do, what are your interests, what are you fascinated about?"

How easily she could let him go off that topic surprised him. Probably, that's what the girls are so strong at, letting go.

"Do you mean my passions?"

"Not exactly. There are always a few things that we want to experience, not our passions, not our goals. What can we call them, maybe natural flings?"

"Yeah, I get you", his eyes glowed, "I would love to fly, to see the world from above, from a different perspective". There is enthusiasm in his voice while talking about these, "That's one of the reasons why I love drones; I could look at the world from above while I'm still on land". He is looking at the horizon where the sea and sky meet.

"That's a nice thought, to look at the world from above."

"Hmmm. So, what do you love to do?"

"I don't have such dreams; I love dogs and own a few. Taking them to the beach, walking along, and talking to them is what I love, and I do that quite often."

"Well, I love dogs too. We think we own them, but in a short period, they own us. Such lovely creatures. Somehow, I think we don't deserve dogs though. Humans don't deserve to be loved unconditionally".

He ensured he didn't sleep for the rest of the date. They drove for a long time, and he saw no skyscrapers around. He asked her the same, and she said with pride,

"Oh yeah, we don't have many skyscrapers here, except for the office or commercial buildings. We are happy with a single-storey house. We aren't complicated people, perhaps."

What she said made complete sense. Everywhere he had been in Mau, all of them seemed to have an individual house which didn't exceed two storeys with a parking space for one or two cars. There are houses with no vehicles but not without dogs. It is nice to see people who enjoy their lives. Their work-life balance is excellent. Everyone leaves the office after 5 p.m. and will be at work by 8 a.m. No one works; they don't even think about it during weekends. Even the general stores, shops, and shopping malls are closed Sunday afternoon. Such is the lifestyle one should wish for. To work the week and to spend the weekend. Not owning anything in excess is one of the most significant forms of freedom. He realised why the beaches are so busy on weekends: everyone is out there, enjoying their natural resources responsibly.

He asked her, "I know a guy who owns eight dogs. You people are obsessed with dogs, aren't you?"

"I don't think it's wrong to be obsessed with extended family."

She dropped him off at his place and asked him,

"Did you enjoy it?"

"The lunch?"

She is disappointed, "Nah, the date." She picked herself up from the pit of disappointment and said, "Well, it isn't right to call it a date. Should I say, did you enjoy the sleeping ride.?"

"Please, cut me some slack. It was a date, and I did enjoy it. I'm sorry I didn't dress properly, slept off, and didn't tell you, my story. I will make up for it some other time."

She smiled, which looked like a smile of contempt. She got inside the car, and just before leaving, she said,

"I don't care what you wear as long as you wear your smile. You didn't do that today. So, I don't call it a date," and she drove off.

He realised she was right. It wasn't intentional, but he didn't smile throughout the day. Probably, he hasn't been smiling for a long time. He couldn't remember when the last time he had smiled. But there was no one to notice that; no one had time to see his smile, rather the absence of it.

J

Krish reached the classroom late in the afternoon and saw her having lunch alone, like every day. He goes from behind and held her from behind.

She turned around swiftly, "Huh, finally… I missed you so much. You didn't even tell me that you're coming today. I have been…."

After 12 minutes

"Say whatever you've to say now," he said, smiling.

"Shut up, I couldn't breathe"

"Well, use better words; you could just say, '*You took my breath away.*'", that sounds romantic.

"This is a classroom; what if someone had caught us kissing?"

"Darling, I say this with the experience of an adult and the ignorance of a teenager: Most of the teenage romances start in the classroom. The community of teachers is used to it, I guess. And had someone seen us, it should be their decency not to disturb." He winked.

"Things don't run here the way they do in your Hollywood movies."

"I am afraid I've to agree with that."

"You seem to have enjoyed your trip while I missed you here."

"My brain was working, but the heart was seeking you all the time, irrespective of what I was doing."

"Which movie is this line from?"

"I watch a lot of them, can't keep track of them anymore" he smiled.

"Don't dare to smile. Six days, and you didn't even care to text me once, at the least."

"I will make it up to you. Let's spend some time together. Talk to your mom and tell her that you will not be accessible for a day."

"Not happening."

"Do you want me to talk?"

"Shut up. I will talk to her tonight, but I am unsure about persuading her. She had never sent me anywhere without company."

"Tell her that I will be alongside. She trusts me; I guarantee you that she will agree."

"You should have been born 200 years earlier, I guess."

"Why? Am I so old-fashioned?"

"Well, that too. But more for your self-centred and your self-confidence levels. You should have handled a kingdom."

"I don't know whether that's a compliment or a comment, but I will take it anyway."

"And where would we go?"

"Does she need to know that information, too? Will she accompany us or what?"

"Shut up. Even if she doesn't want to know, I want her to know."

"Okay then, I will let you know once I get to know."

"You haven't even thought about the place, yet you're sure about my mom agreeing."

"It's not about where you go, darling; it's about who you go with."

"I wish we were at some private place."

"For romance?"

"To slap you, idiot."

"Thanks for respecting my integrity and not slapping me in public." Krish smiled.

10

"Why do you keep listening to the same music, boss?" asked Robin, looking at Acharya's playlist.

"Do I? I've never noticed. Perhaps I find something new every time I listen to them," he replied.

"Is this how you escape answering the questions?"

"I listen to all kinds, new and old, but a few are my favourite, and they are repeated in loops. And, before you ask anything, I never get bored of them."

"I do that too. I listen to a few songs hundreds of times and then get bored."

"Happens."

"Happens? Is that all? I didn't tell you a secret about my music-listening inability to get this one-word response in return. I want to know how you do it without getting bored."

"First thing, it's not a secret; millions of people do that, listening to the same song till it starts irritating. Well, let me share my secret. I associate music with people, locations, things, and situations. Whenever I listen to a song, I remember one of these: a person, a place, or some part of the past. The lyrics run in the background while I re-live that particular thing. Initially, I felt that one should never associate any song or music with people or places because when they leave, or when you leave, that music will keep hurting them, but you know what? I was wrong. One should always associate a form of music with everything because though you lose them, you can still keep them with you in the form of music."

"But isn't it again a foolish option? To re-live those moments again?'

"Why is it so? All of them don't need to be bad. It is a choice anyway; you decide what you want to remember. If you think there can be painful moments too, there will be, and pain is inevitable anyway."

Robin shook his head and immersed himself in his work while Acharya returned to his music.

XI

"I want him here; he has been good for us. All the staff members are used to him, and they prepare themselves to work around him accordingly. We have been collaborating perfectly, with clear communication among the technical and functional teams. I don't want to have someone new start afresh and build the bond again between the employees." The client manager was on the phone with someone from India.

"Talk to him; if he agrees to stay there, I don't have any issue from our side", Dhiraj responded.

Sanjay entered the technical room, "Hi Santhosh, I've heard from your manager that you will be leaving for India in another 15 days."

"Yes, Sanjay, I've been assigned 90 days of work here, and I'll leave finishing the same."

"But buddy, we've been working together so well so far; why do you want to leave? We can look into any concern that's troubling you"

"No, Sanjay, you've treated me so well. I'm glad to be part of this assignment; I've enjoyed my time here. I love the way you people balance work and life. It's a pleasure working here. But just like every time, all the good things should come to an end. I promised to be here for 90 days and have my commitments back home. They need my presence there".

"How about visiting us back in another month or so?"

"Sanjay, this means a lot to me. To be loved by you and your team, the assignments might not work that way. The one replacing me will take care of everything I've done, and once I'm gone, returning in another month will require a lot of unwanted paperwork. Technically, don't worry, Sanjay, the one replacing me, will ensure all your expectations are met".

"It's a pleasure hosting you, Santhosh; I wish we meet again," Sanjay said blankly. His disappointment in not winning the argument/discussion is visible.

Santhosh is happy, realising his work is worthy, acknowledged, and appreciated. His responsibilities are handled as expected, and he has set the tone for the upcoming teams. He could make an impact, and that's all he wanted when he came here. The satisfaction of reaching your expectations is too sweet.

Right after their discussion, everyone in the room began staring at him. Now, they all know that he will be leaving in another 15 days. He didn't care about anyone except for the expression on Sarah's face, which didn't look good. With a bent head, she looked up with broad eyes and no smile on her lips. He felt frightened. He was not bound to any commitments, yet he just felt scared. They all started asking him about the replacement guy coming and his capabilities of handling everything that'd been set. Sarah didn't say a word, though. That worried him even more. The absence of the words hurts and scares us more than the words.

When no one was around during the lunch break, she sternly asked him, "So, you will be leaving in 15 days. Is that fixed?"

"Yeah, tickets are issued."

"When are you coming back?"

He paused a bit before answering. At that moment, he wasn't sure whether he should try to come back or not.

"I don't know for sure, maybe after three months or so, just before the go-live (the deployment of the product to the real world is called a go-live)".

"So, you won't be coming back."

He is perplexed by her straightforward statement. He knew that he wouldn't be coming back unless there was an emergency and unavoidable requirement. He didn't say a word. He is ashamed even to look at her.

"Don't give false hopes, ever. Don't promise things you can't keep, which you don't intend to keep. Let the people deal with the truth rather than the hope."

"I'm sorry; I didn't mean to make a false promise. That wasn't my intention."

"Intentions should be visible in your actions, Santhosh. No one cares about your intentions; they judge you by your actions."

He didn't want to prolong this because he had indeed lost credibility there. There aren't many worse things than losing the credibility of your words and actions.

K

"What did you two people discuss?"

"Why is that a matter now? You're here, and we're going; that's all that matters."

"Nah, I want to know the secret, to use it again whenever I want to go out."

"I told you, it's about whom you're going out with. And I just told her that you're my responsibility all the time. From when I pick you up to dropping you back at your doorstep."

"She trusts you more than she trusts me", she expressed sadly, almost seeming like she was admitting a fact.

"That's not true; she just believes I'm more mature, and that's not the point. Do you have any idea where we are going?"

"No, as long as you don't ask me to drive, I don't care."

"Okay, how long can you sit on a bike?"

"I don't know, the longest I ever did was around 2 hours."

He is a little worried and it's visible on his face.

"What happened?" she asked, and as if she could read him, she said, "It's okay, we will take breaks; I can manage long distances, I guess."

"I hope", he is still a bit worried. "If you can't manage, I need to make it up for this too, again."

"Well, in that case, I'm unsure whether I can manage, " she grinned wryly.

They reached the hill station after travelling for over 8 hours, and starting early in the morning was a good idea. They crashed onto their beds and didn't move an inch until late evening. He is the first to wake up to see her sleeping like a baby. He kissed her gently on the forehead, and as she didn't even realise it, he kissed her cheeks too.

About half an hour later, he tried waking her up while she still craved those extra minutes of rest. He sat down, pulled her onto his lap, and whispered into her ears. The stars are out, and there is a *pani-puri* stall nearby. He knew she might not fall for the stars, but the *pani-puri* would surely hit, and it did. Though the god of laziness still drags her back, she manages to pull herself up. He waited while she got herself ready, and they both embarked on a small walk.

Over time, things and methods become obsolete, and experiences become clichéd. In recent times, stargazing has been categorised as a cliché. But just like kneeling while proposing, holding hands while walking, honeymoon post marriage and amateur romance of teenagers, some sayings still hold their importance, their fragrance and freshness even after centuries.

After eating stomach full of *Gol Gappes*, they walked for forty minutes before sitting on a bench at a roadside park beside a lake. Unlike the movies, it isn't a full moon day. So, it was pretty dark by the time they were there, but that seemed to be the perfect time to be. They both sat quietly, staring at the distant horizon, the hills on the other side where small lights pierced through the darkness with no intention of winning it but to express their identity. She slipped her hand into his without looking at him, and he put an arm around her shoulder, pulling her closer. Like every other hill station, this one has also comforted its locals to sleep early into the night. Only the tourists are on the roads sparsely. It is getting colder every minute, and the darkness is slowly swallowing the cloud-capped mountain range on the other side as the household lights go down one by one. She is moving closer to him, not allowing the chilly winds to get between them. He felt the warmth of her breath on his neck, and before he could turn towards her, her gentle lips touched his. While the twisted lips were caressing each other, his hands went around her waist, pulling her even closer, feeling her chest against his, and they stayed there, in that state, for a long time without any idea about the passing time. For them, the time froze there along with them. While most of the town is deep in their dream worlds, these two are submerged in their dream world, a world of romance and serene oneness.

After a long time, while walking back to their cottage, there was nothing around them, or at least for them; nothing around mattered. They just walked, looking at each other, smiling, without uttering words. They hadn't spoken to each other in over an hour, yet everything was alright.

That is probably what love is: being able to share the comfortable silences.

She is the first to spark a conversation, "We might need to eat quite some food now."

"Why?" he is surprised that she is talking about food after that romantic evening, "hungry?"

"Hungry, yes. But I read somewhere that kissing costs a lot of calories." She smiled.

"Well, maybe, but I think the regular amount of food should be enough because if kissing costs a lot of calories, all the couples should either be very lean or not kissing."

"So, this is it, then."

"What is what?" he is confused.

"This is your talent, spoiling the romantic conversations with a simple line of analysis."

It pricked him a bit to realise what she said was true. He felt terrible for spoiling the moment abruptly. So, guys, note it down. Play along with the romantic conversation when the other person is in it. Moments rarely come, and don't waste them just by bringing in your intellectual analysis, especially when they're unnecessary.

11

Robin finished reading *Call Me by Your Name* by Andre Aciman and exited the terrace after dinner. Acharya is already there, blatantly staring at the stars.

"What are you looking at, boss?" Robin asked.

"The stars, I own a set of them." Acharya is still staring at the stars.

"Why is love so cruel, Acharya?"

"If I had a nickel for every question I answer you, I would have had another set of mirrors and books at my store, Robin."

"Why does everything trace back to the store?"

"Only if I had a nickel every time you ask me a question, man."

"Come on, boss."

"You don't know that. You're assuming that love is cruel, and you may give me everything you read about love, but you haven't lived a love life or experienced it. You would talk about a lot of failed or successful love stories. Still, you have no idea how it feels to look at someone and get lost in time, how it feels to kiss a girl, ignoring the world around you; you have no idea about the beauty in lying to people just so that you can spend a minute with your girl and a lot more."

"What?"

"Love isn't cruel. It is hard, for sure, but not cruel."

"Why is it hard, boss? Why does it have to be hard?'

"Because it doesn't have any rules."

"I beg to differ, but I'm sure you would have an explanation. Please enlighten."

"When you go on a highway, you overtake the vehicle in front without any problem, assuming that the one in front will indicate if they need to move out of their lane. That's the rule, and everyone knows and follows that. We created rules that apply the same way worldwide, and then we have tests to give one a license. But that doesn't apply to love. There are no universal rules in love that are applicable around the world. The rules created are often specifically applicable only to that particular couple. Love is some bond where you can bypass all the expectations either by reaching them or by not reaching them."

"It makes sense now. We often think it's difficult to follow rules, but it is tough not to drift away when there are no rules."

"True that."

"Now, it makes me believe indulging in love is very dangerous. One must be prepared for unknown rules that will appear out of nowhere. Sometimes, irrespective of how much you try adapting, it still breaks you down."

"Only those things you love have the power to break you, and they deserve it. I already told you that love is hard, and the statement 'I love you' is not very far from 'I may break your heart into pieces'. But you know what? There will be a few people who deserve to do that. You just need to make sure the person who says it gives you enough strength to live with the broken pieces."

"But Acharya, how can I match her? I mean, when I see the way or the intensity with which she loves, I know that my love would never be enough."

"That's a bit tricky, Robin. There is no way to measure love; it is tough to decode what is wrong when something goes wrong. You can't say one way is right or the other is wrong. Everyone has their ways of loving someone, and you can't prove that is right or wrong. Not only you, no one in the world could. There is nothing more abstract than love."

"I don't understand whether you're making me feel comfortable about love or pushing me further towards…" he ended abruptly, opened his phone, and began typing something. After a few seconds, he finished the sentence, "philophobia."

"What is that?"

"Fear of falling in love."

"Check for the word which describes the fear of being in a relationship or maintaining it?"

"Surprisingly, it's the same word, boss."

"Then, you're already experiencing philophobia."

XII

The penultimate weekend of his assignment has arrived. He didn't want to get out of his bed. He wanted to stay alone and not do anything for the whole two days, not to be bothered by anyone or anything. Late in the afternoon, he got up and walked along the roads around his place. The serene surroundings on a weekend evening in Mauritius are a place to get lost, to slip away into the world of emptiness, the void. Probably, that's enlightenment, to feel nothing, to have nothing to worry about, to be unaware of the world around you. There was a ShopRite store (ShopRite Trianon) nearby where he stayed, where he ended up. That is about to close, too. He walked in swiftly to buy a chocolate cake from the bakery named 'Ogu' (If you ever happened to be in Mau and fond of cakes, this is a must-try). He ordered a 1.5 Kg cake and has to wait a while for that to be delivered.

While pacing up and down without aim, he saw a girl who seemed to be sobbing, sitting alone at a table. She looked Spanish. He went up to the table and said,

"Can I sit here?"

She nodded.

He sat there quietly for a while before saying,

"If it makes you feel any better, I'm a bigger loser."

"Sorry???" she is startled.

"You've been sobbing for quite some time now, but I guess I deserve to sob more. So, it's unfair for you to be leading the race."

There is a forced smile on her face.

"It's my father's anniversary, and I happened to be here alone while my family is grieving in Granada. I know it's strange that people wish to have company in grief."

"It isn't strange, not a bit. We always need someone to share our feelings. Let me know more about your father. Let's grieve together if you're okay with it".

She explained him how her father was a member of the Spanish Marine Infantry, and because of this, they had the best resources and respect from society. Even though he often had to leave them (she and her brother) without any explanation, he always made sure to make up for it every time he returned. Two years ago, he was KIA during an operation, and all the information they were given was that it was a "Special Operation". Though the national government is filling all their needs, it just couldn't fill the void of his presence.

He listened patiently without interrupting, and at the end, he smiled at her.

"I'm sorry if I've burdened you with my story, but why are you smiling?"

"There was a proud feeling on your face while you talked about your dad."

There is a wry smile on her face, "That's all we're left with; we need to carry his legacy, the pride".

ORDER NUMBER 131.

"It's nice meeting you. My order is here; I got to go."

"Thank you so much. It's nice to have someone by your side while you're sad and heavy in the heart. You came out of nowhere for me; I'll remember this for a long time. Can you give me your number?"

"I would love to, but I only have a company-provided mobile number, which I can't share. Let's keep it this way. Remember me as an unknown guy, a stranger you don't even know the name of, listened to you and know your story while many people you know don't know any of that."

She got up, hugged him, and kissed him on the cheek.

"Oh, come on………." he exclaimed

"I'm sorry. Did I make you feel uncomfortable?" she was taken aback by his reaction.

"Oh, no, no, no………, strange things are happening to me on this Island: a date earlier and a kiss from a Spanish girl. My friends are not going to believe either of these. Anyway, Now I perceive why Spanish is one of the most romantic languages."

"Enlighten me, too, with your claim." she smiled.

"Because that's been spoken by people like you. It comes off lips like yours."

"Don't you think it's too soon to flirt?" she asked, smiling.

"Maybe, but I read somewhere that a guy should never miss out on any chance of flirting."

"Is it so? And where did you read that?"

He smiled sheepishly and answered, "I wrote that on my wall to read it daily".

ORDER NUMBER 131. 1.5 KG CHOCOLATE CAKE IS READY.

"You ordered for a 1.5 kg cake? All for yourself?"

"Ha-ha. I don't sob when I'm alone and sad. I eat cake," he said, smiling at her and leaving.

She realised that while listening to her, he was battling something of his own. Yet he could stay still and pay attention to every word she said. She felt the broken souls were beautiful; they survived despite the odds and helped others improve. With such a big cake, how long is he going to battle melancholy?

L

They returned to the hotel and sat in the lobby, enjoying the warmth and escaping the cold weather outside. He told her he was going to the bookcase in one corner beside the hotel's front desk. She looked around and smiled. After reading the summary of one of the books, he pushed her to the dining area for their dinner.

She didn't eat much as she was still full of the *Pani-Puri*s she ate, but he had a full meal while listening to her stories. By now, he had gotten so used to her loud speaking that he hadn't noticed anymore. They returned to the room, changed into their nightwear, and walked to the terrace. The top floor of their hotel has an open terrace with no lights, but the candles are arranged here and there just so that you don't trip over things.

He is the first to walk to the terrace, allowing her to change her clothes.

"I will be on the terrace; they have an open top. Join me if you're fine with it, or else, rest here. I don't mind a bit of personal space too." He wanted to be there alone, reminiscing the whole day. That's what he often does. Irrespective of how the day goes, he sits quiet and isolated during the night and thinks of everything that went through the day just so that he can look at the situations from a third-person point of view, outside the box.

"Okay." She replied coldly. She sounded disinterested.

He went atop, already slipping slowly into the nearest past. To be specific, to the time of their passionate kiss. He had no idea that the day, or should I say that the night, was going to get so better. He is looking at the sky for no reason, enjoying the cold breezes surrounding him in all directions. He looked at the half-moon and wondered,

"Why are you the most desired pet of poets? What do you have to offer them? Though it's called moonlight, that light isn't yours."

But before he could think of plausible answers to the questions he posed, she was there, in her shorts, walking towards him, shivering a bit already, but all his eyes were concentrated on her shoulder, from where the guitar was hanging. He got onto his feet.

"How did you…. Where did that come from?" he is still surprised.

"It was just beside the bookshelf that you showed me in the morning, idiot."

"But I didn't see it."

"Yeah, the heart only sees what it wants to see."

"Oh! I got the patents for the movie lines, but that was a good one." his eyes are still fixed on the guitar.

She played her favourite songs first and then his favourite songs. He sat there without making a move, admiring her artwork. He noticed that she wasn't shivering anymore. The desire to express her heart through her art gives enough warmth to the body. Probably when the heart is satisfied, the body doesn't feel anything. Presumably, she entered a different world with a guitar in her hands. After playing more than six songs, she is about to wrap it up.

"What are you doing? Are you done?"

"Yeah, happy now?" she is close to furious.

"What happened?"

"I played over six songs, and you didn't say anything. I don't know whether you liked it or not. It seems like you are hating it. You stood there, idle without even looking at me."

"I was enjoying it. I was submerged in it. I wasn't looking at you because I didn't want to make you uncomfortable. But I loved every piece of it, every second."

"You do this all the time. I don't even know whether that's true or not. You didn't need to compliment me but should've acknowledged it. Anyway, thank you. I borrowed this only to play for you. I need to return it to the desk."

"I'm sorry", he meant it. You can see it on the face when someone means their apology. "I didn't mean to disappoint you at all. I admit it; it is a mistake not to acknowledge it. I do. Can we please continue?" he urged her.

"I'm sorry, I am out of that flow and phase—some other time. I'm tired and feeling cold, too. Shall we get back to the room?" she wasn't angry, but she didn't seem happy either.

"Yeah, sure. I will wait for that some other time." he is disappointed, but there is nothing he can do. "Let me submit that at the desk. You go and rest," he asked for the guitar. And just when he was about to go down, she pulled him and said, pointing to the sky, "look up, a star has just fallen".

He smiled and left to submit the guitar back. By the time he returned to the room, she fell asleep. He looked at her, smiled, and stared briefly before going to the bed. Even before realising how tired, he is dragged by the goddess of slumber into her hands.

12

Robin took a day off from work to visit his mom, and on the way home, he thought of everything Acharya had told him about love. Though he got himself inclined towards Acharya's philosophy, he brushed it aside, telling himself that it was just a form of manipulation. But at a corner of his heart, he knew he wanted to believe in what Acharya said because he didn't try to preach or persuade them but just told all of them just like he was sharing his experiences.

"I heard that you're in town. Can we meet?" Srishti called Robin.

"Where did you hear that from?" Robin is not answering the question.

"From BBC. Stop evading the question."

"Will see; I will decide after a meeting."

"What?"

"I will have a meeting with my conscious and subconscious committee members. Will do as advised by them."

Srishti is impressed by his way of escaping the questions, but then, she needs an answer. She has been waiting to meet him, and he isn't visiting home often anymore like he used to. So, she didn't want to miss the opportunity. She also has a lot of questions piled up for him. Robin probably also knows that, so he escapes to answer the questions.

"I will wait at the college ground. Come there around 4:30PM." Robin texted Srishti.

"Why there? Come here. Mom wants to talk to you, too."

"Home? Some other time."

-------------- 4:20 P.M, Same Day------------

Robin is early. He sat there watching the college students playing sports. That was the place he used to visit as a kid. Every day, after school hours, he would go with 5 of his school friends to see the college students playing games. The ground was reserved for college students, but Robin and his friends waited there every day, trying to play alongside them. All those people, all those days, everything came back to him. When you re-visit a place, you re-visit the time.

"Oh, now I understand why you didn't want to come home." Srishti came early, too, but not before Robin suffered the nostalgia.

"What? Why?" Robin isn't looking at her.

"Because you can't watch these kids playing cricket from there. You self-centred idiot."

Robin laughed. "Hold on. I didn't know that there would be kids playing here. It is just a coincidence."

"Here. Mom gave these."

"What are all these?" Robin is opening up things. He knew there would be sweets because Aunty knows that he likes them. Except for her father, everyone from Srishti's family knows about Robin almost as much as Srishti does. Her mom likes him so much that Robin talks more to her than to Srishti.

"What is this?" Robin asked her.

"Ghee, homemade. I told her that you like it."

He smiled, "And how come you invited me home? Dad?"

"Dad is in school. Being the head of the department comes with its disadvantages."

"Gulab jamun is nice; pass my feedback to Aunty."

"Yeah. You give feedback to everyone except me." The tone suggested sarcasm, but the words are facts.

"What feedback do you need?"

"Nothing. Just answer a few of my questions."

"Shoot."

"Why don't you want to live a regular life? I mean, just like everyone else."

"Because I don't approve of those methods. Education, employment, marriage, kids, retirement. I wouldn't say I like that order. That template may promise satisfaction or assure guaranteed happiness, but I don't want to go down that line."

"What is wrong in following the pattern?"

"It's tempting to follow a template, Srishti, but you won't have your trademark."

"Okay, so, the trademark with your template doesn't have marriage?"

"Marriage is a pandemic that's been accepted and left untreated for centuries."

"How about we live together for a few years, and then, you decide whether you want to follow the template or not or, even better, have your trademark by making changes to it."

"It won't work out, Srishti. This discussion happened before between us. I told you why it won't work out. We grew up in two different worlds.

After living 23 years of your life one way, you can't change it immediately into something else."

"But I am saying that I am willing to."

"It is not something just you can try, Srishti." Robin is turning impatient.

"But why?"

"Because you have no idea what you would jump into. You are not aware of the depths of struggling life." He was about to shout but controlled himself.

"I am ready for the challenge." She is instigating him with every sentence, and she knows it. But there is no other way to get him to talk about his feelings.

"Okay. What do you know about hunger? You might have felt hunger while fasting, but you don't know how it feels when your empty pockets silence the screams of your stomach. Because poverty isn't a prose to read, isn't a poem to rhyme, isn't a point to understand but an unwanted product of ineffable greed. Do you know how it feels when a dream breaks? Knowing that something you want very badly will never be yours? Did you ever meet a person whose dreams were broken as a kid because he couldn't afford the support he wanted, though he deserved it? If not, meet someone. No one is more dangerous than those people. With me, life would be a pack of experiences tangled with risks. You wouldn't be able to do things you want to. You would need to compromise even for the most common things." Robin's voice changed over the statements. There was genuine suffering that was visible in his eyes and his voice. Srishti got what she wanted: an explanation. Even if she hadn't, she wouldn't have dared to go further with his discussion in that mood.

Robin hates himself every time he meets her because of how it ends. It always ends with him being on the emotional side; he doesn't like it. He doesn't want to raise his voice or hurt her, but that's how they end up every time they meet. And for the same reasons, he decides against meeting her, though he knows he wants it too.

XIII

He is glad he got a 1.5 kg cake as it turned out to be delicious. While he is busy enjoying vast chunks of it, the phone rang, and it's Sarah.

"Hey, do you have any plans tomorrow"? Sarah seems to be in a hurry while asking him the question.

"Are we going on another date?"

"Does your answer depend on mine?" she sounded impatient.

"Calm down, I am free. I don't have anything on the calendar."

"That's good. Get yourself dressed by 9 a.m., we're going somewhere". There was some excitement in her voice, which he noticed. It's rare for the guys to see nuances, but he did in this case.

There is nothing more exciting than the combination of certainty and uncertainty. After the call ends, he knows he is going somewhere but doesn't know where to go. Gradually, the cake didn't seem as tasty as it was. He put that aside and started thinking about the probable places. He pondered over a lot of things for ample time before failing to figure out any destination. He just hoped that she wouldn't take him her home.

Anxiety has some relation with time. Depending on the context, it goes either too slow or too fast. The Sunday arrived, and it was almost 9 a.m. He was ready way early and was sitting at the same window looking at the blue sky, similar to the time before their first date. He could see her car from there and got down before she could park it. She is about to take her mobile phone out to call him, but he is knocking on the glass.

"Where are we going?"

"This isn't a big country like yours; you will get to know very soon."

He understood there was no point in requesting her because he was sure she would not give away the details. So, he turned towards the window to enjoy the view. Half an hour passed, and the road appeared familiar but vague. He figured out that it was the road to the airport.

"Are we going to the airport?"

"Yes"

"I still have to stay for 15 more days here."

"I don't want you here."

"What about my luggage?"

"Those six pairs of formals and those shorts and tee-shirts? I will parcel them."

"Most of them look the same, but I have 13 pairs of formals."

While he was waiting at the entrance door, sheepishly staring at the departure door security, she parked the car and ran towards him.

"Come", she dragged him towards another side of the airport.

"I didn't bring my passport or anything?"

"Did you bring your wallet?"

"Yes"

"Then, kindly shut up and follow me."

Now, he is more worried. He did bring the wallet, but there wasn't a lot of cash in it. He does have an international debit card provided by the organisation, but that nervousness is kicking in. He doesn't know where he is heading, and she is hurrying him somewhere as if they're late for an undercover mission. Finally, they were at a gate where she showed the security some papers. The guard asked for his identity, and he showed one of his Indian Identity cards. Guard let them in. They're in the airport but didn't enter through the usual doors people use. He is dragged somewhere through the basement of the port. His nervousness is growing minute by minute. Her stern face is only adding to it.

Now, they are out on the runways, picked up by a jeep, and are going beyond those runways. So far, it all looked like a secret mission. She showed some papers to the security there again, and now they're being picked up by a guy in a jeep who is talking into a walkie-talkie.

"Is everything clear? Are we permitted the pad?"

"All set; reach there through the northwest passage."

"Copy"

The equipment inside the jeep also looked suspicious; he couldn't perceive what was happening around him. He looked at her with hope, but she was as plain as an expensive painting, which we don't usually understand. After controlling his anxiety for a long time, he turned to the officer driving the jeep for answers.

"Sir, where are we headed?"

The guy turned towards the girl sitting in the rear seat and smiled. He turned back and was about to say, but his walkie-talkie buzzed him.

"Cap is on his way to the pad. Reach there and wait for permission from the control centre."

"Copy"

The officer turned to him and said, "Don't worry, we're almost there. You will see for yourself".

M

She is late to the class again, as usual. But then, irrespective of when she enters the class, she sits there next to him. It's a fixed structure that no one disturbs in the class. The chair next to him is always left vacant. We have no idea whether the others in the class did that on purpose or just chose their regular chairs, but somehow, they sat next to each other every day.

"Only 20 more minutes" she whispered.

"Of course, if you come 30 minutes late, there will only be 20 minutes left."

"Whatever. Shut up and concentrate on the class." She replied and turned to the other side of her best friend. We all know when a girl says a best friend, more than 90% of the time, it is a guy. They both chit-chat throughout the class and get caught more often than not.

The class ended, and in between the sessions,

"Why do you people continue with your chit-chats even after getting caught?" Krish questioned them.

"Because once a great man said, "Never give up and never accept defeat" "her best friend, Balu, responded.

They both had high-fives while Krish had a face-palm.

"So, how did your trip go?" Balu asked him.

"It was so good", they both responded simultaneously and looked at each other.

"Yeah, sounds believable." he laughed and went out running.

"Here", Krish has an envelope in his hand, "take this and read it when you're at peace."

"Love letter?" she smiled with her eyes stationed on the envelope. "But with no chocolates? Poor presentation skills."

"I belong to the club of old-fashioned youth", he smirked, "We think the insides matter more than the appearances."

"You seem to be the head of the club." she pulled the envelope out of his hands and placed it carefully in her bag, "I will read it in the evening."

....

He returned from lunch to the class to see her standing outside the classroom talking to a guy. He went straight ahead into his chair, waiting for her.

"You seem to have forgotten who that is. He was the one who misbehaved with you the first day of our college." his anger is visible, both in the tone and on his face.

"No, we became friends while you were in Sri Lanka. He is not all bad."

"You may forget what happened, but I can't and won't like seeing that happening."

"You don't want me to talk to him?" she is inching closer to the argumentative state. "Are you telling me not to talk to him?"

"I am saying that it hurts me to see you smiling along with him. I can't forget that incident, and I'm reminded of the same every time I look at him. It disturbs me a lot to see you with him."

"Hey, it's just a talk. He just asked for my number."

"And..."

"And what? We exchanged numbers."

"Okay," Krish is distraught and doesn't want to prolong the discussion.

"Please... don't make this an issue." she is not angry anymore, but he is.

"I didn't want you to talk to him, even for once, but now, he even has your number. What do you want me to do, celebrate the disappointment?"

"I'm sorry. I didn't know that you wouldn't like it. I won't repeat this, but what do I do now? I already gave him my number."

"Tell him to delete it when he texts you." he is very blunt and instantly realises that it isn't appropriate. "It won't be easy, just don't respond. He will understand eventually."

She said nothing, and the afternoon session went as quiet as a crocodile moving for its prey. They sat at their regular end-of-the-day spot, the bench at the library where they wait every day for her bus to leave. There are no words, just silence, but that isn't a comfortable one. He didn't say anything, and just before she was about to board the bus,

"Love you," he said in a shallow voice.

She smiled and boarded the bus. She didn't turn around to say bye. He waited until the bus turned the corner, and there was no sign of her turning around. She got a text right after the bus took the turn,

"Read the letter sometime. See you," his text read. She would have forgotten if not for his reminder. She is still thinking about him controlling her actions. During their afternoon discussion, she felt suffocated, as if he was taking away her freedom. But his text brought her back from the thinking world. She opened the envelope to find a small piece of paper on which something was written. It wasn't printed but was written carefully, word to word, with precision.

Not always are we capable of expressing our feelings; perhaps that's when most of us stare at the sky to align our depths with the stars and the universe. We often think we're stargazing but have no idea how often the stars gaze back at us.

If Stars gaze back, they would've witnessed a pleasant pair having a rare yet highly tremendous discussion not long ago. They would've seen the strength of two dissolved souls, two broken hearts that stitched each other—a pair of brains tired by the mediocrity around, a team that repaired each other together.

That night,
No tears shed,
No fears spread,
No prayers read,
But a lot of unsaid words are heard.

The stories that you stirred,
With those strings that you played,
The songs that you sang,
All those hidden bells that you rang,
Everything seems to have fallen in place, darling.
Hey, starry sky,
She did that for me,
Lucky you, witnessed it for free.

Neither does she blemish your past,
Nor does she promise you a future,
It's only the present that she presents,
And there is nothing more pleasant.

Yo girl, you broke my walls,
Yo girl, you increase my smiles,
For you, I walk an extra mile,
Yo girl, you fill my dreams,
Yo girl, you kill my fears,
Yo girl, you double my cheers,
More than anything, you raise my standards of love.
I love you.

Those stars, they owe us for our night, we must have made their day. So, in return, as an acknowledgement, a star had fallen. You remember that, don't you?

How about the next time we name a star our own, and any time we don't get to see each other, we have a look at the sky and let's feel being next to each other?

She finished reading the letter and re-read it twice. She lived those moments again and got off the bus smiling. For the first time, she seems to have experienced a complete day. The day started with the excitement of the previous day, from their trip and then went into a disappointment in the middle and ended with a smile—the reason behind all those three being the same person. But then, she didn't know that was what life was made up of. Excitements, Disappointments, happiness, and sadness all come together, but the most important thing is to balance them. Some days end on a positive note, and some don't, but you have to be there, patient, waiting for your chance to do something about it. Life isn't as unfair as it's often depicted; it's unjust only when you don't grab the opportunity you get and when you don't give your 100% for something you believe in.

13

"Robin, you're back already?" Acharya mumbled from his room.

"Just now. I tried to avoid disturbing you, but you still sensed it. Your senses are working very well, old..." he was about to say, old man, but refrained from it.

"Old man. Finish the sentence, young man. It's okay to be aware of your age at times. I used to think it was the stupidity of the human race to celebrate a disease called ageing on every birthday. But with time, I learned that celebrating birthdays can also mean celebrating one more year's knowledge, experiences, and memories. And you were saying something."

"I was saying that your senses are working very well; you must be a very happy old man compared to your contemporaries."

"That's the tricky part there. Having good working ears when listening to gossip is nice, but it hurts when your neighbours are noisy. It is good to have a keen eye when doing research, but it gives a bad impression when observing a person. It is so beautiful to have a fast nose when sitting in a restaurant looking at the food coming towards you, but it hurts so much on a day when you're fasting. So, young man, everything has its pros and cons. When your senses work better, you suffer more."

"I have a new short-term target now."

"Which is…"

"To win an argument with you."

"I never argued with you. I never said whether you're right or wrong. I only tell you what I believe and think, which doesn't need to be right. There is no right and wrong, Robin, only actions and consequences."

"I read this line somewhere."

"Yeah, me too. When you sit in a library or a bookstore for so long, you get to read a lot of books, but over time, you tend to forget who said what, but you remember the lines which make sense to you when it's personally related to you."

"Admit it, boss, forgetting the names can also be because of your age."

"Well, maybe, but I'm damn sure the names were not as big as the lines I remember."

Though Robin was beaten again, seeing the sarcastic Acharya after a long time felt nice. They have been involved in many discussions off-late, which are very philosophical. Not that Robin doesn't like philosophy, but he loved sarcastic Acharya. His wit felt more appealing to Robin when it was used to silence someone with just one sentence. Paragraphs of philosophy are exciting and profound, but one-liners are fascinating and hot.

XIV

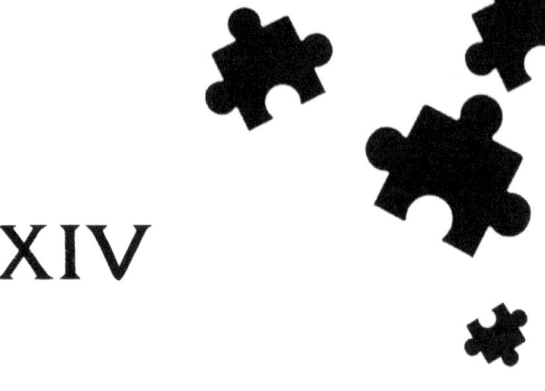

There stood the beauty, a 10.30-foot-tall and 42. 45-foot-long Bell Jet Ranger (turbine engine powered) helicopter. A five-place copter (including one pilot) is not a beast but a beauty. Probably, the helicopters are female, at least this one. There are a lot of curves to it. This lightweight, twin-engine copter sits on the pad, capable of flying at 220 kmph at its maximum weight. Well, it's called a bird, but it looked more like the Nemo with its pretty red and white striped canopy. I forgot that I was standing in the centre of a helipad without knowing what I was about to do, but the beauty of the copter relieved him of the nervousness.

"What's happening? I'm nervous."

"I can see it; it's painted all over your face."

"We got 90 minutes. Because it's two of you, I need to make it clear; decide who gets to sit in the cockpit because that's where you'll get the best view from," the pilot said, who had just reached there.

"It's him; he will sit beside you", she replied quickly, even before Santhosh could fathom what was happening around him.

"Good for you, man; let's get in there", says the pilot with a smile.

After we got in, he gave him a headset and checked the controls. A few minutes later, he started explaining,

"Look at that lever positioned between your knees; once we are in flight, you need to press the knob on it to speak, and you should speak into the headset microphone. We must communicate only through that and remember to keep the knob pressed while you speak. We will be covering the whole of Mauritius from above in the next 90 minutes. And is this your first time in a helicopter?"

"Yes," he realised he was going on a helicopter ride over this Island nation, a chopper ride. He dreamt of a chopper ride many times, especially when Uber offered chopper rides in UAE, but never even in his dreams did he think he would go on one. He looked at her, sitting in the back passenger seat. She smiled and said,

"So, that's what we're doing. Don't be nervous and enjoy these few minutes."

"Oh, is this a surprise?" the pilot heard her and responded, "I promise you that I'll make sure that these 90 minutes are worth remembering for a long time, if not forever. Are there any preferences which you want to visit?"

"That underwater waterfall" she replied.

"Here we go", and the rotor started chopping off the air to produce the flight, and the pilot pulled back the cyclic stick between his knees to direct the chopper.

We travel by flight, but this is an entirely different experience. We don't get to see what the pilot sees in an aeroplane. But here, seated in the co-pilot's seat, I could see exactly what the pilot felt and saw. The bottom of the cockpit, under your feet. It is made of glass. So, except for the canopy, the whole cockpit is made of glass, giving the best view of anything from the front and the sides and even beneath your feet. I understood why the pilot made it a topic about the co-pilot seat even before boarding.

All the places Santhosh visited in the last ten weeks are being revisited. He didn't like that earlier, to see the same places, but this time, he is loving it. He looked at the 108-foot Shiva sculpture in Grand Bassin from above. For a moment, even the god seemed to be beneath him. The sugarcane fields, mini-islands, immaculate beaches in the North, the capital Port Louis, Black River Gorges National Park, Chamarel, Alexander waterfalls, Cure Pipe, Tamarin, Flic en Flac beaches, and a lot more places that he visited over the last two months are all seen from above. Though every place holds its speciality and importance, Le Morne stood apart from all the others. That's where you get the view of the underwater waterfalls. The pilot took them precisely above the spot, and said,

"This is the best view you could get to see this. Enjoy your minute," and hovered the chopper there for a while.

The visuals are unreal. When he heard the name (underwater waterfall) for the first time, he imagined how it might look, but the scenes are nothing like that, nowhere close, yet stunning and fiction-like. The colours from the top differ significantly from what we see on land.

Different shades of the blue of the sea and the mixture of that blue waters with the sand on the shores are nothing short of a feast to the eyes.

He cannot decide which is more exciting, whether the view from above or the ride itself. Bikers may understand how it feels to bend their bike at a hairpin bend going at over 100 kmph. Now, imagine being airborne where you can see 180 degrees around you, going at over 150 kmph and bending your vehicle entirely to one side; it's almost like a rotation over its axis; it's just ineffable. He cannot contain his excitement, but at the same time, he doesn't want to miss out on anything around him. He is mesmerised by the capability of the human eyes and how they can help the brain store all those vast visuals within microseconds. But it's not the time to think about the extraordinary faculties of the human body or the fantastic quality of the evolution process of humans. It's his moment to cherish, breathe in all the aroma, grasp the whole horizon, and store all the details of the visible nature while hanging between the land and the sky.

N

"How does this dress look on me?" Prags asked Krish, who was already looking at her in awe. She always wears western, which suits her so much, but after looking at her in a traditional outfit for the first time, he couldn't get his eyes off her.

"You should try traditional more often; it looks so good on you", he responded, still staring at her.

"Click a good picture, then".

Krish is happy to have a picture of her in traditional attire. He is getting ready with his phone.

"A good one, please; I need to send it to him", she said, adjusting her stole.

"Who him?"

"The guy who gifted this dress. He was my classmate in the school."

"Oh! Did he present that on your birthday?" his tone changed slightly.

"Why would I wait this long had I got this on my birthday? he was in town recently and bought me this a couple of days ago."

"Gifted? For no reason?" his mood is shifting; he isn't calm anymore. He is turning impatient with every answer.

"Yeah, he likes me." She is looking at the pictures he clicked and checking out the one to send, in which she examines the best, "So, he got me this."

"He got that for you just as a friend. Is that what you're saying?" he is significantly upset.

"Of course, we're friends. He proposed to me a long time ago, but I rejected it. We're just friends. He has no intentions now; it was a long time ago." She is still busy sending him the photos.

He smiled and said nothing.

"Why are you quiet? You don't believe me, do you?"

"Did it ever occur to you that once you love someone, you can never unlove them again? You may hate them; that's a different story, but you can't unlove them."

"So, you are saying that he still loves me, and he has intentions behind gifting me this?"

"I can't speak for his intentions, but he still loves you. He may not have presented you the dress to get to you somehow, but your acceptance of it keeps his hopes alive. I'm happy for him because the satisfaction of having hope and the thought of still having a chance are the only things that keep the one-sided lovers happy. I'm happy for him, but not at the expense of me being hurt. Yes, it sounds selfish, but that's what love is, the most selfish bond on this planet."

"Not everyone is like you, he gave me this just as a symbol of friendship, and that's it. Hemanth knows about him too, and I showed him this dress in the morning; he liked it too."

"You are still in touch with Hemanth?" Krish is now confused about what to be upset about.

"Yeah, we talk daily, and I don't wear any dress without showing it to him."

Krish couldn't say anything; he sat there disappointed.

"Ok, tell me this: do either of them know that you're in a relationship now?" he asked her calmly without letting his frustration take control.

"No, I didn't tell them. They don't need to know".

"What do you mean they don't need to know; they need to know" he almost shouted. He calmed himself and said, "Sorry, that was impulsive. Now, listen to me. Let me tell you, from a guy's perspective, we never lose hope. We may break up but cling to it unless we move on. We are waiting for one moment, which may help us bring it back online. So, if they don't know that you're committed and doing everything as usual as you did when you were single, that sends them mixed signals. You might not know what they feel, but I'm telling you, that's not right. Moreover, why didn't you tell them that you're committed?"

"We never talked on those lines. It never popped-up in a discussion." She doesn't seem comfortable with the discussion.

"And I forgot, why do you need to get approval from Hemanth for every dress you wear? And does that mean he gets to see you every day before I see you in the class?"

"I didn't think of it that way. We're used to this. I used to show him everything I wore when we were together, and it's just continuing."

"Continuing after moving on, and even after someone else is in your life. Do you think that's fair?"

"What do you want me to do?" she is angry now. The anger that took over the inability to win the argument.

"Either tell him that you're committed or stop talking to him," he said firmly, with a stern face.

"Why are you so worried about him?"

"It's not about him. It's about me. I want to be your priority. I want to be your go-to guy. Yes, these all sound very amateur and selfish, but I feel that's what love is about—having someone to hold on to, being everyone for that person, and seeing everyone in that person. It would be best if you didn't talk to many people because I want you to miss me. Yes, I want you to be independent, to stand on your own, but when you need support, the first one to appear on your screen should be me. I want to be that guy who is always on standby for you. I don't want you to move close with any of the others because I don't like to see others getting a share of the love I deserve. I know this might pressurise you, but when it comes to love, I'm as bad as a child, seeking all for me, selfishly."

14

If not for their terrace talks, they would have slept in the shop for the majority of the days. They are similar in how they like to have their day. It is quiet, peaceful, yet productive. Neither ends their day without reading something; the topic doesn't matter. Both start their days with a 15-minute quiet session where they get up and do nothing but stare at their phones. Acharya goes through the news that he misses out at night, and Robin checks the messages he misses. There is a generation gap, you see.

Robin is knocking on Acharya's door as it's already time for them to get to the shop.

"I am leaving, boss. Will unlock the doors for our employees." After understanding Acharya, Robin is also referring to the shop as *ours.*

Acharya opened the door and said, "Wait for another 3 minutes; I am joining you", and closed the door behind him.

Within that short time and space when Acharya opened the door, Robin's eyes went through the wall in front of him, which was immaculate but a poster right against the door. That would be the first thing anyone sees when they open the door.

"Adios am'ego'" is written in block letters on that poster. It attracted Robin, but he wasn't sure whether to ask about it as he sneaked into the room, which he wasn't supposed to.

Both left for the shop, and Acharya settled into his chair at the corner and started writing something like every day. He keeps writing something throughout the day in a small notepad of his, which is kept away from everyone else. Robin found him reading a particular book, too, now and then, which he held along with that notepad, locked up in the desk. Robin has always been curious about what he is reading and writing but never tried to ask, assuming that would invade his boss's privacy.

Robin thought enough was enough during their lunch and brought up the topic.

"See, I know I shouldn't have, but instinctively, my eyes went to the wall and saw the poster in your room. That unsettled me so much that I couldn't concentrate on work properly. I want to know what that poster is about, and even if I didn't want to, I would need to. I hope you understand."

"That poster is the last thing I see before leaving the home and the first thing I see after entering the home. I guess you know that's just morphed Spanish. *Adios* means goodbye, and *amigo* is a friend."

"Yeah, I understood you are saying goodbye to a dear friend, ego. I want the story behind it."

"I have been egoistic all my life and realised very late that it isn't helpful. Since then, I have been trying to put an obsolete board on my ego, which is very hard. I started this mission of eradicating ego from my life over 30 years ago, but it is only as successful as our population control."

"Oh, that's what our staff talks about." Robin smiled, "they say that you're the epitome of the representatives of ego and self-centredness. Either I didn't experience it personally, or your wit overshadowed it."

XV

Santhosh sat quietly for a very long time on their return journey, sitting in the car, possessed by nature. He didn't move in his seat for long, staring out the window at no particular object. It's strange how eyes could fathom a lot of information in microseconds and, in the same way, how they could ignore another lot even while looking right at them. His eyes are open, but he isn't looking; he lets all that beauty sink in. He painted a lot of colour books as part of his school curriculum as a kid, but he can't recall any colours that were as bright or as beautiful as the colours he witnessed today in just about 90 minutes.

"So, are you going to talk any time soon?"

She pulled him back into the real world, "Sarah, this is something I have never done; I want to remember every moment. I know there might be many people who do this daily, but even for them, the first flight would have been special."

"So, how do you feel?"

"Oh! Not everything can be explained." he is still in the aftermath of a surprise.

She smiled.

"Trapped in the nervousness, anxiety, and surprise circuit, I forgot to thank you. Thank you so much. This means a lot to me."

"I know it does. You told me earlier that flying is one of your wildest dreams. I couldn't give you wings or buy you a drone, but I could make you fly for 90 minutes."

"I can't thank you enough. I used to wonder what the birds are so excited about every day in the morning; they wake up with the Sun and then make noises all the time. But when you can look at the world from above every day, why won't you be excited to wake up early in the morning."

"Well, not all pilots would agree with this", she replied sarcastically.

"Please tell me how much the trip cost you."

She looked offended. "An hour's journey from the North to pick you up. Try repaying that." The voice was a bit loud, and the face was red.

"I didn't mean to..." he stuttered because that's precisely what he meant.

"Well, at least, from now on, mean what you say."

They reached his place, and she stopped him before he said goodbye. She got out a box of items and handed them to him, and said,

"I know it may sound stupid, but I love you. That box contains chocolates and two pendants for you and your mom."

Before he could concentrate on that "I love you" part, she diverted him to the box, but he wanted to stay focused.

"You don't even know me; how are you sure that you love me?" he sounded severe and intense

"I don't think people know each other much before being in a relationship, except for the ones who are long-time friends. Two people often fall in love, understand each other, come to harmony, and live together. I've known you for over 70 days, and I feel that's adequate to decide whether you're the one I could suffer with."

It sounded very logical, and he couldn't think of anything to say at that point,

"Give me a few days, and I'll answer you."

"What? I didn't give you a question paper; I only expressed my feelings about you. You are not bound to say anything unless you want to. Anyway, remember the date. I haven't told these lines to someone before."

"19th of November, I'll never forget. For many reasons", he recollected the Spanish Kiss, the chopper ride, and the proposal now.

He was told what was inside the box, but he was still curious about how those would look. A pack of Ferro Rocher, two tiny pendants, one labelled 'S' and the other with the Hindu symbol of 'Om'. Although she said he did not need to answer, he knew he would need to, eventually. Why is life so hard? It is just moments away from his best experience. Now, he needs to think about answering her. Chocolate can make things better. Probably, that's why she gave him the chocolates so he could think and decide in peace. He opened the Ferrero Rocher to celebrate the golden experience and began worrying about the proposal though she stressed that it was not a proposal but an expression of love.

O

"This movie is boring, let's leave", Prags whispered in his ears.

"That's what you said the last time, too," Krish looked around the class, submerged in the movie's plot.

"Because that was boring, too. I don't understand why the course includes watching these boring movies," she is irritated.

"They aren't boring. They aren't commercial ones, that is all. They're called the parallel cinema, which are apart from the mainstream commercial movies." He gave his 2 cents.

"Okay then. Parallel cinema is boring."

"Well, they're not everyone's cup of coffee. But a lot of them are stunning pieces of art."

"I don't understand why even Balu is so interested in this. Is it only me who doesn't like this?" she asked him genuinely.

"Seems to be, yeah." He looked around and responded genuinely, too.

"Okay. You finish watching it. I'm leaving."

"Where will you go? And alone?" he forgot to whisper this; his classmates stared at him for breaking the meditation-like tranquillity of the class, but immediately after realising that he was talking to Prags, everyone went back to the movie, glued to the screen. He continued, "You need to watch it anyhow because we need to write reviews for these movies."

"I will do that somehow, later. Just tell me whether you're coming with me or not?" she is impatient.

"Wait for another 15 minutes. We will leave". He didn't want to leave after the whole class stared at them.

They went straight to the canteen, leaving the class 45 minutes early.

"You aren't letting me watch any of the curriculum-prescribed movies." he meant it.

"Did I force you to come out? Go back now. Don't blame me for this" She brought out her weakness, her anger.

"Shut up; we both know I won't let you go alone." He responded with a disturbed mind.

"Please go back. Please finish watching your movie and come. I don't mind; I will wait here."

"Not happening. Tell me what you want?" he asked her, pointing at the ice creams.

"That orange one." She grabbed it from his hands and said, "Now, return to the classroom. That movie is more important for you anyway. I don't want you coming back at me for spoiling your movie mood."

"It's over, and enough with the drama, queen." He tapped her head. "Enjoy the ice cream, and we will wait for your bus."

He is sitting there, waiting for the bus, but his soul is still running in that classroom, close to the big screen. He is a man who admires the arts.

15

Summers: Summers in India. Summers in South India and then Summers in Chennai. This is the order of efficiency of the sun in ascending order. Though illogical, Chennai seems closer to the sun than other places on earth. It feels as if Sun loves Chennai so much that he tries to kiss it every summer.

"Boss, the guy who declared that water has no taste either never been thirsty or never been in Chennai." Because of his experience in construction, Robin was asked to supervise the shop's renovation. He was in the sun helping the workers, explaining how their boss wanted it to be reshaped. "Only 2 hours passed?" Robin is surprised to see the slow passage of time. It happened only when he was in school and while during planks. Never has the time passed so slowly.

"Speed of passage of time is directly proportional to the amount of human enjoyment." Robin chose the language of mathematics to express his frustration. "It passes quickly when we enjoy it and very slowly when we struggle. I guess time senses our need to move fast or slow and puts only one task in its task list to do the exact opposite of what we want.

"The only way to eradicate its effect is by living it," Acharya told him without lifting his head off the book he was reading.

"Oh yeah, I read it and heard it many times. Live every moment."

"Yeah, live every moment not because it passes slowly or quickly, but once it is passed, it is past. There is nothing you can do about it. That's the beauty of the past. The first thing is it's over, and the second is you can't change it."

"You seem to have some unforgettable past. When are we going to discuss that, boss?" Robin is attempting to dig in.

Acharya brushed it away with a shaking head decorated with a smile.

"Someday, boss, I will get that all out."

It is that time of the day when even the sun is tired. He was done for the busy day and left for home to rest in his wife's lap so that he could return tomorrow rejuvenated. It seems that everyone has their responsibilities including the Sun, and people don't like you, irrespective of whether you handle them or not.

Like every day, they sat on the terrace staring at God knows what but sat there quietly, as people in meditation.

"Do you believe in God, Robin?"

"In his existence or his ability?"

"That is an excellent question. Out of those, which one is a bigger question for you?"

"They are relative, boss. But for me, the question is, does that matter?"

"Care to elaborate?"

"I don't think about his existence at all, boss. Whether he/she/it exists is completely irrelevant because I believe we don't need him/her/it to live our lives. All we need is each other. That's what I believe in, and so, I don't even give it a thought when it comes to his existence."

"How about his ability?"

"God is only as strong as teenage love. We can always move on." Robin smiled. Acharya is stunned by his way of looking at God and Love. He didn't derogate either of them individually but compared them.

"What do you think about all the devotees, prayers?"

"I like to not think about them, boss." Robin is nonchalant. "Your turn now. What is your version of God?"

"Ineffable Robin. Lots of gods. The ones who pass their wisdom to you, share their meals with you, make you laugh, and much more. But if you mean a supreme power by God, I believe God doesn't have enough time to look after all of us. So, it's on us to look after ourselves."

"So, you do believe in God's existence?"

"I am not sure about the non-existence, Robin. That is all."

"Then, what category do you fall under, boss? A Theist? Atheist? Agnostic?"

"Humane."

XVI

"It's been a pleasure to host you here. On behalf of the whole team, I thank you for your efforts and the time you've given us. I hope you enjoyed our company as well as Mauritius. Let us know if you have any of our girls in mind so we can get you married and keep you here, making you, our son-in-law. Even though we wish that you stay here longer, your priorities come first for all of us, too. We all hope to see you again," Sanjay toasted on behalf of all his staff at the send-off meeting on the eve of his departure.

It's a tradition that the client has followed in Mauritius to send off the employees with a party, be it a dinner or an evening snack treat. It was a team of over 30 people, and in those three months, Santhosh developed a bond, with almost every one of them being the only point of contact for any technical issue. They all wished him good luck for the future, and almost everyone asked him the same question, "Did you enjoy Mauritius?". Tourism is such an essential factor for them. They cared about what the visitors felt about them, their country, their behaviour, and their helping nature.

Just when they're about to call it a day, nearly around 5:30 pm, Santhosh stood up at his place and said,

"Thank you all for bearing with me all these days. Thank you for caring for me and not letting me feel inferior among seniors, even for a day. Thank you for treating me equally and special at the same time. Thank you for making my experiences memorable. I love the way you people work and maintain the work-life balance. I love your lifestyles. And yes, I did enjoy Mauritius, maybe even more than many of you do. It's a great pleasure working with all of you. All my frustrations during this period were only with the work; none were with your personality. You are all beautiful in and out...."

"So, tell us about your crushes in this room", his colleague shouted from the other end of the table-a few of those called along.

"If I revisit this place, I will surely discuss that. I hope to meet you all again soon".

Before leaving, he texted Sarah, "After office hours, let's meet at the waterfront if you're okay with it".

"Do I have a choice to hear from you again, if not now?" she responded.

"I'm informing my cab guy to leave without me", he texted back.

Le Caudan Waterfront is a commercial development in Port Louis, the capital city of Mauritius—a place where shopping malls, cinemas, restaurants, and pubs are located. A small area was allocated for the people to enjoy the pleasant evenings facing the water. She came running to him while he was waiting for her for a while now. He almost forgot that he had been waiting.

"I'm sorry, an urgent piece of work was thrown on my face at the last minute." she sat beside him.

"That's okay, a lot of important things come to us during the last minutes." he didn't even turn his head.

"So, what time is the flight? In the afternoon?"

"Here are the pendants. I ate the chocolates you gave me. But I can't take these things home. I can't have them with me."

She received them, "You have played well. Instead of telling me this right away, you dragged it till the last minute so that I didn't have any chance to try at anything. You are worried that I would have tried something else had you told me this earlier, aren't you?"

He is sitting stoically, without showing any emotion. After a while, he answered, "I didn't think it that way, but I was worried what if you are offended with me returning these pendants, after which we would have to go through a lot of uncomfortable silences during the last days of my trip. So, I postponed it, and I'm sorry for that".

"So, you don't love me. Do you have clarity on how you've come to that conclusion? I mean, not because we are from different nations and it won't work out and all other reasons like those, but are you sure you don't love me?"

He kept quiet for some time, thinking he wouldn't have felt good kissing that Spanish girl if he had feelings for Sarah. He likes her; she gave him the best memories but not love. He answered, "Yeah, I'm quite sure".

"Fine then, but you're yet to answer my question."

"What question?" he frowned.

"What time is your flight?"

"I'll need to report at the airport by 12:30 PM".

"Okay, inform your driver not to pick you up; I'll drop you at the airport."

"Ha-ha, nope, I've one strange airport journey experience with you, and let's keep that intact."

She didn't find that funny and even looked disappointed, "just to say goodbye one more time, to see you for a few more minutes than everybody else. Don't you feel I deserve that?"

He felt sorry, but there was no way he could express that, "You deserve a lot more; I'm just not good at these goodbyes, Sarah; I can't handle them properly. I wish to be alone whenever an emotional situation occurs. Leaving Mauritius is an emotional moment for me, and I want to deal with that all by myself. This is not about you, Sarah; it's about me".

He even refused her to drop him home that evening and wanted to go by public transport. She dropped him off at the nearest bus stop and told him what bus to take to reach his place.

"Thank you for everything, and more than anything, for understanding me".

"One of us has to" she said.

He boarded a bus, and when he was about to slip into deep thinking (people usually call that sleeping), the middle-aged man sitting beside him started a conversation.

"Hi"

"Hello"

"You don't look like a native. Are you from Bangladesh?"

"No, you are misfiring Sherlock Holmes," he wanted to say, but he said, "Nope, I'm from India."

"Nice, so, are you here for work?"

Santhosh was surprised. "How did you know?"

"Ha-ha, it's easy. You are not on your honeymoon clearly, and solo tourists choose other places over Mauritius."

Santhosh smiled and thought, "Well, Sherlock isn't bad".

"So, what do you do for a living?" stranger isn't cutting off the conversation, disturbing his state of deep thinking.

"Oh! I suffer," Santhosh replied; he is keeping it as short as possible.

The stranger laughed, "We all suffer, mate; what are you good at?"

"I'm good at a lot of things, but what I do most often is cancelling the plans at the last minute; I'm very good at that",

The stranger hesitated and said, "You don't seem to be in a mood to talk, my friend. I'm sorry; I just wanted to indulge you in a conversation to make you feel better, as you looked slightly disappointed with something."

"I'm sorry, I work for an MNC. I'm here on an assignment, and I'm leaving tomorrow. Thanks for the effort, but I would love to deal with it all by myself, sir. Thank you again." Santhosh replied with a blank face.

P

"How do you manage to take me out on treats? How do you arrange the money?" her eyes glittered with curiosity when she asked the question. He doesn't often see her eyes filled with passion; that happens only when she talks about her new clothes and her interest in modelling. People glow with a different brightness when they talk about their passions, don't they?

"Why do you want to know?" he pulled her by her hand, focused on the road they were crossing. He crossed over her to keep her away from the traffic on the road. She noticed it, smiled and looked at him, eyes filled with love, which he sadly missed as he was still glued to the traffic. "It's a secret I can't reveal."

"Ha-ha, you lend money from your brother." She laughed.

Her way of saying it has taken him aback, and his pride came out for a walk after that statement. "Nope. I never did that so far and have no idea of doing it too."

"Then, tell me, please."

"Some things are always better left unexplained, unexposed, and inexperienced. This is just one of those. I will let you know when the time comes." He thinks rhyming, zigzag, or confusing words can convince the females better than straightforward answers. "okay", she says reluctantly, disinterested in prolonging the conversation.

They reached the mini restaurant just a few minutes from their campus, outside the gate. She planned to visit it before it became famous, and he obliged just like any other boyfriend. He had gone to his hostel room the previous night and solved problems for the students, which earned him some money. That's what he does; the online platform **Chegg** helps him make money for his dates with her, which sometimes turn expensive. He sits out a few hours the previous night and earns enough to take her to a movie or a restaurant. **CHEGG** is a platform where students worldwide request solutions to their problems, and one can register to solve them. If you provide the keys in the desired formats, your answer gets approved and paid accordingly. So, all the middle-class boyfriends out there, if you ever thought that education doesn't help your love, here is proof that it can. Concentrate on your studies or skills; someday, they will come to your aid. That's his secret, which he didn't want her to know.

"So, what do you want to eat?" she asked him, going through the menu card.

"Whatever you order." He replied.

"Oh please, Mr. Drama King, stop it."

"I have a logical explanation behind my emotional statement above. But I promise that you won't like it."

"What is it?"

"Based on our past dates, you will order 3-4 kinds of items, of which at least one turns out to be a flop. On average, you eat only 60-70% of the good items, and the flop ones go to a place my mom usually calls a dustbin: my stomach. So, I'm just waiting for your order to eat 30-40% of those good items and most of the flop items. So, as I said, whatever you order, mam."

"Your logical explanation is stupid." She didn't want to admit the facts he explained.

"I told you, you wouldn't like it," he laughed.

The law of averages wasn't kind to him this time. All the items were tasty enough, and she gave him a nasty look every time they tasted one.

"Done, or do you want anything else?" he asked her.

"I'm full. I am not a bulk-eater like you." Her response came at lightning speed and kind of woke him up.

"Do you have any idea about the number of calories you've gained in the last 2 hours?" he waited for her to finish eating so that he could ask this question.

"Did you go to any defence training camp?" she shot back with a completely irrelevant question.

"Nope, I didn't. I couldn't. I tried to appear for SSB, so I tried several physical and mental as per the requirements but couldn't attend the test for several reasons." He suddenly became enthusiastic about explaining his attempt and then returned to reality and remembered what he had asked. "Don't divert the topic. Answer my question".

"I asked you because this is what my dad (an ex-defence officer) does. He takes me to any place I want to go and allows me to do whatever I ask for even though he doesn't like it, but once that is done, he makes me feel guilty about it. I see you doing the same. You never said no when I asked you to take me to this place, but after coming out, you're asking questions about the number of calories. Not just that, you have many things in common with him, especially regarding these disciplinary activities. You remind me of him a lot of times." She is turning a little emotional. Her dad died a few years ago, and there were a few times when she mentioned how much she missed him. She continued, "Earlier in the day when you pulled me to the other side of the road, my dad used to do that. He scolds me passionately, which I see when you scold me, too. He doesn't let me eat the junk much; neither do you. He makes me sit and explains many logical reasons and mature ways of looking at life. You do this more than he did. I hate you both for this reason. But more importantly, why do you want to make me feel guilty about what I did rather than explain why I shouldn't do it in the first place?" she was emotional during the speech. Yet, she recovered and is now very curious about the answer to her last question.

"Do you want a one-liner or an explanation?" he is up for the task.

"You will explain anyway, even if I say I don't want it. But how are you always ready with the answers to any question I ask?"

"Regret and guilt are the bigger and worse feelings than failures."

She waited for a second and then, "That's it? No explanation?"

"You want the explanation?"

"Nope I don't want it, but I need the explanation." She sometimes sounds smart.

"Had I told you that it's not recommended to go there, you would've had many other questions and might not have trusted me. But now, after experiencing what you wanted, my words make more sense, and you may regret your actions. In the first case, you could only imagine what it would be, but now, you know what it is. I don't want to sound negative, but we all lack imagination. So, regret is stronger than imagination. Experiencing something gives a better understanding of anything than the imagination does. So, I chose this way of teaching something. I don't know why your father did that, but I'm glad to know I remind you of him. I know no one can replace him, but it's an honour to be able to make you re-live moments with him. I'm glad."

"True. Regret is a stronger feeling. I regret asking you for an explanation."

He laughed.

"And you're yet to answer another question. How do you always find an answer to everything I ask?"

"That's not true. I don't have an answer for everything you ask. For example, I don't have an answer to this question of yours. But most of my answers come on the spot because I have a reason behind everything I do."

"I've something to tell you, but please don't be upset about it." She looked at him in a way that suggested something terrible is coming his way. He waited for her to continue.

16

Except for the time while making a sale, Robin sits at different sections of books and reads. He takes out a book, sits in a corner, and doesn't move until the next customer arrives. Being a quick reader, he finishes a book every 2 to 3 days. While all the other employees are just passing the time looking at their mobile phones, giggling and laughing, Robin is submerging himself in the world of words. Acharya noticed it.

"Why don't you write reviews for the books you're reading?"

"But why, boss?"

"So that you spend some time on writing and when you do that, you start analysing the book. We never know what new information or realisations that will bring us. The devil is in the details, Robin, which emerges when we analyse."

"My life would have been easier had you not made sense every time you spoke, boss."

"Compliment coated with sarcasm; I will take it, Robin." Acharya got up from his chair, approached Robin, and put an arm around him. "Start writing after finishing a book, every book. It doesn't matter whether you like it or not; start writing. Also, when you're reading, I suggest you read two opposite genres of books together. Let me explain: if you started reading science fiction, read non-fiction, pick up Indian history, pick up a world history of the same times, if you began reading a book explaining Evolution theory, start a religious book too. Read these parallelly to figure out the patterns, similarities, or points to compare. This is just a suggestion; make sure whatever works for you."

Though his boss is becoming friendly, Robin never expected him to put an arm around his shoulder and surely didn't expect him to explain what books to read.

"But I thought you wanted me to talk to people more than read books. You wanted me to live them more than reading them."

"I still want you to do all that; the more you read, the more ways you get to live. While reading a book, you sometimes fall in love with a person who would have died a hundred years ago. Love can be virtual. Writing is a process of engaging someone's emotions even without knowing them. But the problem is, that's a one-way communication; you can't have a dialogue with them, you can't talk to them, and then, you don't have a chance to see whether they agree with you on a particular thing. Without that, you can never know whether we fall in love with them or keep them at their place."

"So, what do you suggest, boss? Read less or love them less?"

"Read more, fall in love with what you read too, but more importantly, fall in love with a real person, Robin."

"What?" Robin is completely surprised by the advice. "Why is that of prominence?"

"Because Love is 10% Romance and 90% Responsibility, and responsibilities teach you lessons of a whole new level, and it also tests your adaptability to the changing conditions."

"Care to explain, boss?"

"When you're in love, with every passing day, it's like unlocking a new level of the most complex game on the planet. You need to level up every day and adapt to the rapidly changing dimensions. There are no lifelines on this game, though; when the game is over, the game is over. This might sound strange to you as Indian parents ask you not to give up on anything except when it comes to love, but one should never give up on love, especially in love. Because I believe falling in love turns a boy into a man."

"But what if I fail in it?"

"Falling in it makes you a man; failing in it makes you a strong man." Acharya has a wry smile on his face. "Love someone, but don't expect them to fill your voids because the ones you expect to fill the voids will only leave bigger ones. The voids are never meant to be filled with love again. That's where the art comes in. Decorate the voids with words, music, lyrics, paintings, nature, etc. Celebrate the voids because the deeper the void, the stronger the art." Acharya went mute, thinking of all the songs that helped him move through the days.

"You ended abruptly, boss, what happened?"

"Oh, that is normal. Just like these mobile phones, we hang when the memory gets full. We need to clear a few memories, at least temporarily now and then, to work efficiently."

"Human-machine comparison." Robin smiled.

"And there is one more important reason. You're a thinking person; as I already mentioned, thinking brings in a lot of misery. All thinkers' happiness always depends on the people surrounding them. Only someone else's presence can cheer them up. You deserve to have someone around you who can cheer you up."

"If that's true, all the philosophers must have had partners, but it's the opposite; most died alone."

"For someone who could do math easily, the math looks stupid, same with everything. Someone who can handle relationships and emotions easily and expertly looks down at them. They don't like to have them in their life. Philosophers are the best people to get married to, but the problem is they don't choose marriage."

"I read this too, somewhere."

"It doesn't matter where you read it. Understand it, remember it and apply it; that matters."

XVII

"You still have time to cancel your driver. Are you sure you don't want anyone to bid you goodbye? I can take a half-day leave if that's your concern."

"I'm bad at handling goodbyes, Sarah; it turns ugly 9 out of 10 times. I wonder why the law of averages doesn't work with me in many scenarios."

"You don't need to use mathematics or physics to convince or confuse me, Santhosh. It's okay."

"Bye, Sarah, let me know if you ever visit India. You can say goodbye over the phone".

She disconnected the call.

She could sense a bit of happiness in his tone but wasn't sure whether it was because he is going back or because he is getting rid of her. Having an answer with no questions is a tricky situation. As soon as she dropped the call, she dressed herself to work, losing all hope of seeing him off, the lost hope of looking at him for one last time.

He reached the airport on time, and while waiting for the check-in process, he started pondering, "I'm 25; when will I ever learn to handle situations rather than escape them? I've told her not to come to the airport because of my inability to handle love. Why? Because it would remind me that I'm the reason behind her tears? Even if she isn't here, I am causing her the pain. When it's inevitable anyway, why not let her have the chance to see me off for one last time? I'm a coward. What if she hugged me and cried? How would I deal with it? I can't leave Mauritius with a light heart then". He talked to himself for a long time before calming down. With great difficulty, he could convince himself that being a coward is okay. It's so hard to come to peace with yourself when you're rational, but that's important for your internal peace because, if not, it can tear you apart from the inside.

When he turned around to say goodbye to Mauritius while on the escalator, he looked at the departure doors from where he entered, and there she was. On the side of the security check, she is standing there looking through the glass doors. It's too far to see what she is looking at, but he is sure that she is staring at him. She ensured he would feel at least a bit of her pain. Both looked at each other without words for as long as the escalator took him away. Along with the escalator, his self-loathing went up, but his heart was dropping.

She called him as soon as he is out of her sight.

"Goodbye, I'm saying it over the phone."

"Bye, Sarah." he couldn't gather himself to say anything after that goodbye, which sounded like she was shouting in his face. All that convincing himself about being a coward is gone, and he needs to come to peace with himself again, from scratch. There is something extraordinary and robust about the goodbyes. Even though you spend much time together, that last sight holds some ineffable emotions. He wanted to leave Mauritius with a light heart but life had other plans. All she needed to do was show up to spoil all that.

Q

Krish is just looking at her for her to unfold that unpleasant information. In times like these, he hates his ability to think deeply. If there is ever the slightest hint that something terrible will happen, his brain brings in all the things that happened in the last few months and starts connecting the dots, which is very unpleasant.

"I pinged that senior yesterday on Whatsapp; I talked to him."

"Oh," his sixth sense wasn't wrong.

"I saw his Whatsapp status; he mentioned his deceased father. I texted to console him because I know how it feels."

Krish didn't say anything. He sat quietly, staring at the bus she was about to enter.

"Say something. You don't know how losing a parent at an early age feels. He and I share similar pain, so I couldn't resist talking to him." She is justifying her actions.

"Okay," his reply is cold.

She is getting irritated by every minute and moved an inch or two away from him.

"If you don't want to sit, go board the bus." his evening is getting worse and reflected in his words.

"You don't understand me, you don't even try. How do you want me to react to it?" she is back to her regular voice, a few decibels over the average human voice.

"I have a similar complaint. You don't try to understand how I feel." he isn't backing off either. "And not just that, you don't think before doing anything."

"I don't want to think deeply like you and suffer. I'm not doing any crime here; why do I need to think about it?" she moved closer, but that's a way of expressing anger.

"Okay, calm down. Let me make a few things clear for you here. We're in a relationship, which is very different from being single. You've one more guy in your life, and you must move accordingly. I'm not saying that you should change everything, but there are a few things you need to sort out with the one you are going to live with. We've lived different lives for over two decades, and it's not easy to change them right away, but the first step is understanding and admitting that they need to be changed." He went into his explanation mode, "I told you that I'm very possessive, not just now but on the day, I expressed my love for you. You know I don't like you talking to him, and you still did that. For one, it proves that you didn't think before doing it, and two, you didn't care whether that would hurt me, and three, now, we're fighting over a stupid topic because of some 3rd person..."

She interrupted, "But I told you why I initiated the conversation. His post touched me emotionally, and then, I couldn't...."

It's time to interrupt, "Okay, let me ask you one question: why do you still have his number? I remember asking you to delete it long ago. The source of this fight is your discussion, and the source of your discussion is having his number."

She stayed quiet for a second, "he is just a senior, and I didn't delete it. No particular reason."

He knew right away that it wasn't any justification. He realised there wouldn't be any conclusion that would come out of this argument. He didn't say anything and is looking away towards the college ground.

"Okay, I am going to board the bus, bye" she said and left.

He stood there waiting till the bus left, and once it did, he texted her, "Love you". That's their thing, their version of saying bye. He waited for her to express it, but as she forgot, it was his turn to take over the responsibility, and he did.

17

"Where are you?" the message read on her phone.

"Hanging somewhere between excitement and anxiety", Srishti replied.

"Why the anxiety?" Robin got diverted from the topic which he wanted to discuss.

"How can it not be? Everything is to be worried about with you, at least a little. So, anxiety is always a part of it, especially when you text first."

"Ha-ha!" Robin didn't know what else to say. He added a few smileys with that ha-ha in the text.

"So, you didn't know what to say." Srishti sensed it.

"How did you know?" Robin smiled sheepishly.

"We don't talk much, but you show many variations in the little we do. So, let's call it experience."

"Now tell me, where are you, physically?"

"At home. Are we meeting?"

"Nah. Let us discuss over texts."

"Why did you need to know my physical location then?" She is disappointed, which isn't visible in the texts. Perhaps, that's why he prefers texting.

"I thought of a meeting but realised it is tough to get a leave from work again." He lied. Is this very common? Are Guys using their work as an excuse to escape the critical situations they must face?

"OK". She couldn't have expressed the disappointment better than this over a text.

"I hurt you almost every time we meet, yet you ask for a meeting; why?" he took so long to send this as he was scared to listen to the reason. He is scared that he is getting closer to falling in love.

"You mistyped a word there. 'always' seems misplaced by 'almost'".

Robin smiled at the message and felt relieved as the text didn't have anything serious about his way of treating her, but that feeling passed quickly. The relief is replaced by impatience as he didn't get the answer to the question he asked.

"I have yet to get the answer to the question," he replied. His smile and his moment of relief aren't visible in the text, but his impatience is. Perhaps this is how the texts ruin the relationships.

"I don't know. I get excited at the thought of seeing you and being with you. I don't think I care about the aftermath. You make me laugh, too, every time we meet. But the ending is always messed up. I accepted that meeting with you is like a Tamil movie climax, which ends sadly most of the time."

Robin didn't understand what to make out of it. She admitted that it ends bitter but also joyful while it lasts.

"But that's only because you live your life, and we only meet occasionally. If you're treated the same way all the time, and if you're pushed to the corners of dependencies and restrictions, it wouldn't be the same. Whenever I said it wouldn't work out, it wasn't about you but me. It is always about me. I don't think I am suitable for a relationship. I am not responsible enough to take care of a commitment." Robin is honest.

"It is always about you, the self-centred guy. Whether it is something positive or negative, you take all the credit for it."

The discussion has taken a turn from there; both seemed to have missed the track they should be on. Acharya observed Robin smiling at his phone.

"Talking to someone funny?" Acharya asked.

"To Srishti, she is saying that most men are self-centred."

"No comments," said Acharya.

"She also said that one of those self-centred guys must have invented the English language, and she explained with an example. I was laughing at that."

"Please transfer the knowledge, Robin."

"She said that the most unique thing that distinguishes females from males is menstruation, and even that word has 'men' in it."

"That's some criticism, man." Acharya liked it.

"Anyway, the most painful process in the world, it has got to have men in it."

"Did you say that, Robin?"

"No, she extended the conversation and said that too."

"She seems to be smart." Acharya likes word games.

"Yeah, anyone who can produce a bit of sarcasm sounds smart to you, boss. She might have just copied that from twitter."

"Sarcasm is a sign of an active brain, Robin. So, yeah, scientifically, they're smart. And do you know the longest word in English?"

"I can guess a few words, but I am damn sure you have a tricky answer."

"Smiles."

"Because there is a mile between s and s?" Robin cracked it quite quickly.

"See, you're smart too. My school principal told me this a few decades ago." Acharya slipped into nostalgia. "School days used to be beautiful, Robin. Without much…". He is interrupted by a customer before he can go on. That's life, though. Nostalgia might feel great, but that's not where you're supposed to stay long. The present is the priority. You can re-live a moment in the future only if you live it in the present, not by just being there.

XVIII

"Is your honeymoon trip over?" asked Anshul, his colleague cum cubicle-mate cum best friend, if there is something like a best friend.

"Man, I wish it was my honeymoon trip; there were only couples everywhere except in the office".

"Well, you spend all your time in the office anyway, so it shouldn't be a problem."

"Nah, it's completely different from my first assignment this time. Mauritian lifestyle and work-life balance are seriously awesome. I was free during the weekends, and even on weekdays, post 6 p.m., there wasn't much we could do," Santhosh said with energy.

"Good for you, I'm going to Nigeria again", Anshul replied hastily. Still, there aren't any hard feelings as he got used to the Nigerian lifestyle by now as he has been travelling there too often and stayed there for long enough to get accustomed to it.

"Mr Nigerian Ass, get citizenship there, marry a Nigerian girl and invite us all for a party."

"Oh! Please!! I'm not Nigerian, and I'm not marrying any Nigerian; in fact, I'm not marrying any Indian either."

"That won't happen for sure; who will marry you in India?". Anshul is a sweet guy with an above-average height and fair skin complexion. Compared to Santhosh, anyone wouldn't even think twice before choosing Anshul for marriage.

"FYI, my parents are already looking for a bride."

"A Nigerian girl?"

"Mr. Santhosh, you can kindly shut up!"

"Arey, talking about girls, listen, strange things happened to me on this trip. I don't think you would believe me, but anyway, I will share".

"What's the point of sharing it when you know I won't believe it?"

"At least I can get them off my head. I had a date with a Mauritian girl, and a Spanish girl kissed me. There it is!"

"You were right, Santhosh", Anshul replied, laughing, "I don't believe you."

"Utkarsh, do you believe me?". Utkarsh is one of their cubicle mates.

"Don't be senti, Santy; I don't care", he replied.

"I knew this would happen, so I'm prepared to be disappointed, folks, so I'm not disappointed now".

"Mr Santhosh, I repeat, you can kindly shut up", Anshul chirped.

R

"Where are you?" Prags shouted over the phone; the sound to his ears was as good as a slap on his face.

"Just came out of the library", Krish replied with urgency.

"Why didn't you pick up my calls earlier?"

"Would you like to listen to the same answer I gave above, or do you want me to alter?" he picked a very wrong time to bring out his sarcasm. "Hello…"

The line got disconnected.

He called her up.

"What?" the question came as quickly and as fired up as a bullet that left a rifle.

"Where are you?"

"Oh, do you care?"

"The classes are suspended for today due to a strike organised by a community of students. I came to the library as you were yet to come to college and then, I submerged into a research paper, failed to notice your call. Mobile was in silent mode. Let me pick you up at the department."

"Go there and pick someone else up. I'm at the library." she gave the required information, but her voice concerned him.

He is walking down the stairs of the University's central library, briskly putting his books back in the bag. He smiled at her, which seemed to have bounced off before reaching her aura. He ran to her swiftly, still arranging his bag and his mind running somewhere in the library, among the research papers.

"So, what shall we do? We've time till your bus leaves, which I think will happen post-lunch." he is talking to her as if nothing happened so that she forgets that she is angry.

"Let's go to the NDRF Canteen; I want to have a coffee", she replied.

The University is also home to one battalion of the NDRF camp, and they have a canteen where the students are allowed to have snacks.

"I like the coffee here; it's strong." he is grateful.

"Shut up; they don't put enough milk, that is all", she shot back.

He had no counter-argument for that because what she said was true.

"So, you were so busy in the library doing what?" she initiated the conversation after a few minutes of uncomfortable silence.

"I was going through the research papers about a particular topic." His answer came quicker than usual.

"What topic?"

"Travellers and their contribution to the growth of the kingdoms"

"Why?" her disinterest is like overdone makeup on the face.

"What do you mean why?" he is irritated by the question.

"Why are you doing that all of a sudden?"

"Oh, you know my interest in travelling. I got this whim of researching the topic while reading history some time ago, and yesterday, while watching the web series *Vikings,* I remembered it again. A messenger character in the series is a traveller who helps a guy claim the kingdoms around their hamlet. And that episode brought back my thought, which was shelved somewhere in the brain palace."

"I am just waiting for a day when I ask you for an explanation and not regret it."

"You need to wait for very long, I guess."

"And as we have nothing to do, shall we return to the library? I will do my thing, and you can go through all the books on the racks there and read anything that you find interesting. The collection is huge; something might catch your eye." He added.

She didn't even lift her head away from the coffee cup, nor was she sipping the coffee. He never knew that there was this way of saying no to something. But with hope, he waited for her to talk.

"Okay. We will go, but return whenever I don't feel like being there." She talked only after she finished her coffee.

He is happy and began calculating that it will give him at least 30-40 minutes in the library before she gets bored.

10 minutes after they entered the library, she asked him

"Still not done?"

From a distance, the librarian gave them both a stare as she talked in a normal voice, which is considered loud even outside the library and inside; it's loud and disallowed. He made a sign and asked her to sit.

"Are you done already?" he was surprised as she reached the state of saturation a lot quicker than he expected.

"I was done 5 minutes ago but gave you time as you're busy", she smirked.

He is disappointed not because she is bored but because his calculation went wrong, and now, he might need to leave the library.

"Give me a few more minutes; I'm at a crucial juncture." He requested.

"Okay, I will come back." She left from there, going towards the reference section.

5 minutes passed, and

"I am leaving; you come whenever you are done." She left, even before he could listen to her completely. He didn't have a chance to ask about what happened.

Soon after she left, he picked up his stuff and left the library. She is nowhere to be seen in the library premises, and he calls her on mobile,

"Where have you gone?" he is furious but controls it to an extent, respecting the surroundings.

"I am at the NDRF canteen." The answer was firm, like the ones you hear in an interview.

He is already upset about not getting enough time to concentrate on his research, and her behaviour is disturbing him further. She didn't give him enough time to get into his working zone. He was constantly concerned in some way, and he didn't like it when she couldn't understand it. He disconnected the call and ran to the canteen in his rage-driven mode.

"What happened?" he shouted at her, forgetting to respect the surroundings now.

"Why are you shouting?" she shouted back. The irony is laughing at them.

"What happened?" he whispered now, mocking her. His sarcastic side takes control of the situation when he is not cool, and that's not a very good sign when the other person isn't in the mood to take it. She saw what he was doing and didn't answer to instigate him more.

An uncomfortable silence followed for a few minutes, but both felt comfortable afterwards. Not all awkward silences are destructive.

He initiates the conversation as he is the one left with unanswered questions. "Why did you have to leave in a hurry? What happened?"

"I don't like to be in a library—a place where it's all quiet. I feel suffocated. And then, that professor in the reference section shouted at me for not placing the books back at their designated places." She is furious.

"Well, it's our responsibility to put them back where they belong," he said, trying to calm her.

"Oh, don't his responsibilities include not shouting in the library?" she believes she has a point.

"It's not a responsibility but an expected behaviour in a library."

"Did you ever take my side in any situation?" she seems to have been pushed across the border into the kingdom of anger, and her tone changed drastically; not the pitch but the way she asked indeed pricked him. They got up and started walking towards their regular place, the bench at the library.

"Do you ever understand or even think about me or what I want or what would make me feel better?" he lost his cool, "You don't think before doing anything. You know how much I like to travel, and I was researching, yet you couldn't stay for a while there. I leave my movie sessions for you; I come running to pick you up, leaving my book halfway in the library; I never said no to any of the dates you asked for; I do a lot of things just so that I don't hurt you in the process but you, you don't even care to give it a thought. He scolded you because it was your fault; admit it. You couldn't give me 30 minutes for my work to be done and come out without telling me what happened."

She didn't say a word.

He grunted and then, almost whispering, said, "It was my fault to let you take me for granted. I shouldn't have made it easy for you from the beginning. Giving you everything you asked for, including my precious time."

"I didn't ask you to come out. I mentioned that I was leaving and you could come only after finishing." She isn't shouting but isn't talking in a normal manner either.

"Okay," he said and left, walking towards the library.

She is taken aback. She never expected him to leave her in between an unfinished conversation. He had never done that before. The moment he left, something entered between them; we often call it a gap, literally, metaphorically, physically and mentally.

18

"Boss, I have been with you for a few months but have never seen you out of control."

"Well, neither did I see you losing control."

"Trust me, boss, I lose it very often, not just around here."

"So, who is that lucky one, Robin?"

"What?"

"With whom do you lose control and show your real face?"

"I show my real face to everyone, boss; I don't fake my nature."

"That's not what I meant, Robin. We all have few people with whom we feel comfortable, so comfortable that we are ready to expose ourselves. They're the people we love to spend time with and with whom we live. The people we love are the ones on whom we dump all our frustrations;

they often are our pressure releasers and stress busters. The sad thing is that we make them suffer and hurt them all the time because we love them."

All this explanation made Robin ponder over his reactions, and he could remember only one person all the time, Srishti. After a few minutes of silence, Robin reignited the conversation.

"I release my frustrations somewhere, but you have nowhere to go. All your time is spent either in the shop or on the terrace with me, or in your room alone. How do you manage to stay calm all the time?"

"You see me often writing stuff in the shop, that's my way of handling it. Be it frustration, sadness, happiness or any other emotion. When I feel bitter, I write; when I write, I feel better. When people think a lot, there will surely be many demons inside their heads, and when you jolt them down, the demons will be on the paper. They are always better on the paper than up there, in the heads."

"Does that work all the time?"

"It is working now, but it was a different story when I was young. As a youth, I preferred the controversial flood to the conversational drought to satisfy my ego, which caused me a lot of stress. Though I used the discussions to gain knowledge as I learned something new with every controversy I invoked, I later realised that peace is way more important than that. You can also have that information in other ways without provoking someone. After quitting poking at people, peace gradually crept in, even without me knowing. It doesn't mean you should shy away from a discussion, no, but you can always have it in a friendly and official manner. That saves you time, emotions, relations, and peace."

"Were you ever in love, boss?"

"I was, I am, and I will always be."

"How do you handle it? I feel that there is nothing scarier than love."

"What makes you think so?"

"Waves are so soothing and calm when you look at them from the shore, but nothing is scarier when you're under it. Love is just like that. I somehow find it so difficult to handle relationships with expectations."

"There is no relationship which comes with no expectations. Even your parents expect your love in return, if nothing else."

"What about friendship, boss?"

"It is often unsaid, but friendship has a rule, to be there for your friends at all times. I agree that there is no rule book, but everything stands firm when it has a foundation."

"But as you said, conversational drought is better than a controversial flood. I feel that drought of feelings is better than the flood of feelings, which I think results in love."

"But I had my fair share of controversial floods, Robin. I experienced it before leaving it. You may say that we need to learn from other's mistakes, but what if those mistakes wouldn't be mistakes in your case? You never know what one learns or makes out of anything. There is nothing wrong in trying anything which is not illegal or hurting someone intentionally. I am not forcing you, but love is a beautiful part of life, Robin. Live it and then decide what you want to do. Just make sure the other person knows what your intentions are. That is all."

"I feel the pressure, boss. Whenever I say I would try my best, I feel the pressure of a promise. When I get stressed for something as small as that, how would I survive the weight of love."

"Humans evolve, Robin. I feel that you're going to be a pretty good partner."

"Why so?"

"Whims, boy"

"If I ever have a bond binding me, I wouldn't be as free as I am. I might need to think of another person before going for an adventure, and I don't want that burden on me."

"Robin, let me talk your language. Adventures is what you want to do, right? Do you know what the biggest adventure is? Gaining the trust of a person and keeping it intact. Any adventure is a burden, Robin. We choose to pick one and let go of the other."

"But..." Robin doesn't have any defence.

"The problem is that many of us build fence of thoughts around us, thinking that fence is our security, but then it becomes the cage. Neither do you let anyone in, nor will you be able to get out of it. Once in a while, come out of the cage, Robin, look around and try to accept new challenges that you thought weren't worth taking on. You never know before getting in."

Robin went quiet.

"Okay, boss, I admit that this is a challenge I am scared to face, but have you experienced solitude?"

Acharya laughed, "Everyone does, sooner or later. That is why I suggest you experience the sea of love as well because, boy, one day, you will join the lap of solitude, and one of the ways to enjoy it is by introspecting and re-living the memories. That differentiates people who enjoy it and those who suffer from it."

"So, anyone without memories will suffer the solitude?"

"Not necessarily. Not as long as you've things to think about. Solitude is spending time with yourself. For that to happen, you need an active brain with something worthy enough to work on."

"Ok." Robin is quiet. "But how can we identify who is worthy of hurting us?"

"You don't identify Robin, you decide."

"We decide whether to love someone or not?"

"Yes. Love at first sight might be true, but that goes further only when you decide. You fall in love with someone repeatedly, and one day, you decide. That's the end of the uncertain road."

XIX

"Shall we wrap it up? It's 6:30, and it's my first day of work after returning," Santhosh is irritated.

"Why do you always trouble me, Santhosh?" Anshul turned around in his chair, shutting down his laptop.

"Do you believe in God, Anshul?"

"Why is that a matter now? Anyway, I do."

"Good. I trouble you because you're the chosen one. If you still want to know further details, ask your god," replied Santhosh without missing out on any chance of criticising the theism.

"Do you remember what I said earlier in the day?" Anshul asked him while both of them were walking out together.

"You say many things, yet none of them make sense."

"Kindly shut up."

"Okay, but tell me, what was that thing you said earlier in the day?"

"It's the same thing; you've all the rights to shut up."

They left the office around 7 p.m. and entered a restaurant for a drink.

"Sir, this is a candlelight dinner special. Do you want me to light up the candle?" asked the waiter.

Anshul and Santhosh looked at each other, and both of them said,

"Yes, please."

And just when the waiter was about to leave, Anshul called him back and said,

"But we are not gay."

"We don't mind, sir!" he left to bring them the drinks.

They sat there for over an hour bitching about their managers, their onsite trips, work, the quality of the client hospitality, and over everything and anything, they discussed *ADELE*. They both love her songs for some reason and fight over owning her. Well, that's how stupid guys can get. After quite a bit of drinking, they both seem to be a bit high,

"Let's go walking to your place; it's not far", Santhosh proposed, pulling him onto the road.

"It's not near either. I will book a cab."

"Nope, let's take a walk. It's good for you, too, to reduce your tummy."

"Who said I want to reduce my tummy?" Anshul is adamant to walk.

"I did; now you have all the rights to shut up and walk along." Santhosh dragged him along.

After a few minutes of uncomfortable silence and looking into their phones,

"Tell me, how did the date go, and what did the girl say?" Anshul asked casually.

"I slept off."

"On her shoulders? That's nice, man, you had a bit of chemistry then and…"

"Hold on, she was driving the car, and I slept off."

"Is that a luxury car?"

"Why do you want to know?"

"I just wanted to know, if it was, you should have gone to the back seat so that you could sleep peacefully and should have made her feel like a cab driver", Anshul responded with disdain, "Are you crazy, how can you sleep on your date?"

"I'm a fool, Anshul, it wasn't intentional, it just happened, shit happens."

"I agree." Anshul is quiet.

"What? That shit happens?"

"No, I agree that you're a fool. Falling asleep is never intentional. But restricting yourself from falling off should be intentional. You didn't try to stay awake; girls are smart enough to notice that."

"Hmm. She did see a lot of things that day. She noticed that I didn't smile enough," Santhosh answered, looking away and recollecting the complete scenario of the past.

"Now, go home and write an imposition."

"Don't behave like my school teacher."

"Okay then, go home and finish the assigned task."

"What task? Don't behave like my manager either."

"Stop being a whining school kid and do it. Take a paper and write,

"'I'll die single, I'll die virgin' a thousand times and bring it to me tomorrow." Anshul is talking in high pitch now.

"I won't. You're not drunk enough to make me do it, and I'm not stupid enough to do it."

"Do you have a LinkedIn account?" asked Anshul in a different tone, sounding like a professional.

"I do"

"Give me your Phone; we are not connected on LinkedIn. Let me see."

Santhosh handed him the phone, and now, they are both sitting at one of the bus stops while Anshul is busy with Santhosh's phone.

"What have you been doing for so long on my phone?"

"Wait, almost done."

"Done with what?"

"I've posted on your behalf; I've created a job. Here, look at it." Anshul showed him the phone. He posted a vacancy alert from Santhosh's account.

"How can I provide a job? Are you crazy? Oh yeah, you're crazy and high. Show it to me." Santhosh is curious. The post read,

Vacancy Alert:

Experience required: No experience is a primary quality, but 0-3 years is OK, too.

Responsibilities:
- Should be able to understand complex products entirely and be very good at communication.
- Experience in any art is a bonus.

Location:
- Should be able to relocate to different areas based on requirements. (Negotiable)

Employment type: Full-time and emotional.

Salary: Not Applicable

Job: Girl Friend (female)

Eligible and interested people, please send us your resume at. We are so desperate that we will respond immediately.

Note: Candidates are chosen after one month of an internship. During the training, you will be tested based on your patience, communication skills, and ability to adapt to the stupidity and volatile nature of the product.

Santhosh looked at it and laughed. He forgot that it was posted from his account. He looked at Anshul and asked only one thing,

"Why did you mention that we are desperate? People should never know that."

"That's true when you want fewer applications, but when you need as many as possible, people need to know you're desperate. So, now, enough of making me walk, go home, and respond to the emails you receive."

Santhosh's place is another 15-minute walk from there, and he walked all the way, thinking about many things he didn't want to think about. People often say that they drink to forget things, but one remembers everything only after drinking.

S

Every time there is a cyclone along the coast, the people have to work on restoring everything to get everything back to normal. After a storm, it always takes a few days to get things straight to adjust to the new normal. There were a few tranquil days. Though it was serene, it didn't help either of them. The peace isn't always as quiet as it looks. Both of them need to learn how to be at peace with each other, or more importantly; they need to know how to be at peace with themselves.

They sat at their usual place, the bench in front of the central library, facing her bus, which leaves in another 20 minutes. The site hosted many of their lovely moments and their last one, the fight. Now, everything else that happened in the past is fading away gradually while the latest battle is filling all those places in the memory lane.

"I am going by the earlier bus from tomorrow," Prags said.

"Oh, why?" his question lacked the surprise or disappointment.

"I restarted the dance classes", she answered. She left the classes so that she could leave by later bus, giving themselves a few extra minutes in the evening after college. Now, she is back to the dance classes, and their leisure time will dry up.

"Oh", he said, "all the best."

She pulled her phone out of the bag and started window shopping online. He looked at that, and it burned him a bit. He waited for her to stop browsing, but she didn't and he said, after growing impatient,

"We won't have time from tomorrow anyway; why can't you put that away." He said in a low voice. She closed the app and put the phone down.

"I don't think I can ask that of you; you like your clothes more than you like me anyway." He added.

She smiled. It's the wrong time to smile, perhaps. Someone who said that a smile is the best response in all situations is an idiot. Don't try that; it works against you a lot of times.

"Isn't it?" he shook her.

"What?" she was not in the mood even to look at him.

"Your love towards clothes is much more than it is towards me, isn't that true?" he reshaped the question.

"Why do you compare yourself with many things, like clothes?"

"Oh, Is it? Do you remember when you asked me whether I love cricket more than I love you?"

"Yes," she answered as if she were on a call with a customer care representative, answering a yes or no question.

"What is that yes for? Yes for 'Your love towards clothes is more' or yes for 'you remember?'"

"Yes, I remember."

"So, the same way, tell me which is more important, I or the designer clothes?"

"You know I like modelling and so, the variety of clothes is important, but don't bring in the comparison."

He is surprised at her diplomatic levels of dealing with the argument but he is stubborn about getting his answer.

"I know they mean much to you, and that is why the comparison; give me the answer."

"It's time, I'll leave." she got up.

He knew it wouldn't take a minute for her to answer his question, but she was just not interested in either answering or admitting that he was right. After she left, he understood that he needed to vent this all out somewhere. His brain might explode if he doesn't let all this frustration out, some way or the other. On the way to his hostel room, he decided what needs to be done and a decision is made in minutes, in a hurry, and while he is confused.

19

On the way to their lunch, Robin stopped and went towards a weight machine at a store.

"What are you up to, Robin?"

He hopped on the machine and got the weight card.

"I am glad the weight of thoughts doesn't appear in the physical weight boss; I would fall into the obese category otherwise." He said, looking at the card.

"So, how much are you weighing now?"

"Healthy enough to work for you, boss."

"To work with me."

"Ok, boss." Robin stressed the word 'boss' just to indicate that he is still an employee and Acharya is his employer.

They reached home and it's Robin's turn today to take the honours of cooking. Just when Acharya was about to get into his room leaving Robin with the cooking, he interrupted.

"Boss, isn't it strange that people always ask us to keep our heads up."

"Why?"

"The same people say it is the weight of thoughts that keep the people humble, with their heads bent all the time. So, they don't want us to think when they ask us to keep our heads up?"

"That is probably the worst crossover of sentences I've ever heard, Robin." Acharya smiled.

"On a completely different note, a lot of people don't want us to think." Acharya bent down to take a note out from his desk. He handed it over to Robin and asked him to read it.

I heard the birds singing and the leaves rustling to the wind.

I heard the flowing water, the water that's kissing the rocks, slipping down the paths.

I heard the air whistling through the trees and then, I woke up.

I did hear birds but not singing, I heard them flying in disarray, scared by the first bullet that's fired.

I did hear the leaves rustling but wasn't because of the wind, they were the ones stomping under the military shoes.

I heard the water that splashed on the faces to clear the traces of blood.

I heard the air whistling; it wasn't through the trees but through the noses of the guns.

I was born in a forest, among the revolutionaries but what to do,

I couldn't pick up a gun, only a pen.

I can't think of taking a life but only of inducing it into a poem.

I can't march in a line but can match it with a fine line of words.

Words might not hold a value when the war erupts but when the war ends, which surely does, it's only the words that are left.

I was born among the guns and was warned against them by the ones who are holding them.

For me, they all looked the same, the ones with and without uniforms. Both of them called me an informer. Both said they work for the welfare of the people but it was always the people who are sacrificed. When I tried to look at the broader spectrum, I understood that both are just following orders of their superiors without even knowing whom they're working for.

When the first bullet pierced through my shoulder, I had one question running through my mind, is it a crime to hope for peace in a world that believes in wars? But I guess they don't want us to think and so, the next bullet went through my head.

#Stop_Stereotyping.

Robin read the whole note and said, "Boss, it's a fine piece of work. You wrote this?"

"Yeah."

"I loved the way you asked people to think by saying that there are people who don't want and allow us to think."

"I wrote this when I realised how quickly we take sides. Everything has a cost, sometimes it is too huge for the naked eye to see".

"Where did we start, boss? I mean, what were we talking about, where did we start and where are we now?"

"If one could draw it on a board, there would be nothing clumsier than the trajectory of human thoughts. We often lose track of them." Acharya is staring quietly at the whiteboard on the wall in his cabin. He got up and wrote it there.

There is nothing clumsier than the trajectory of Human thoughts.

XX

"So, you think you can arrange a cubicle for me there?" Santhosh is inquiring over the phone,

"Okay then, I will not get any official transfer but I'll work from there".

"Someone seems to be moving out of here," Anshul said without lifting his head off the black screen he is staring at.

"Eavesdropping is not acceptable, you know? Mr. Ass"

"Well, it's the product's behaviour, we can't alter some. Now shut up and say where are you moving to?"

"I feel too comfortable here. This place feels like a comfort zone, I want to move to Hyderabad"

"Yeah, we all know you're not the man of normalcy. Something needs to go wrong for you to be fine. Everything falling in place scares you. You're not an easy guy to understand, not an easy guy to be friends with. I don't understand why you want life to be complex and complicated. What's wrong with having a regular life Santhosh, why are you restless all the time?"

"How long have you been waiting to spit this out?"

"Isn't that a good way to escape the important questions?" Anshul said mockingly, looking at Utkarsh who is sitting at the opposite corner cubicle.

"Hey, don't involve me, you two are a couple, you deal with it" Utkarsh responded.

"I wonder, Anshul", Santhosh took a deep breath, "how humans globally have accepted that change is complex and routine is simple. I feel the other way around. To do the same thing over and over, to stay at the same place for years trouble me, it reminds me that we are staying at the same place while the time is running ahead. I feel most of us are being left behind by time. I don't intentionally make my life complex but I'm not scared to do that. I would prefer facing problems trying something new rather than seeing the same, already determined success results, and performing the same tasks. I don't want to end up doing the routine stuff and blaming society for making my life mundane at the end of the day. And I agree that I'm not an easy guy to be friends with, probably because I'm intense all the time and I bore people with philosophy. I respect you for dealing with me all these years."

"Keep respecting me, I will deal with you for many more years" Utkarsh smiled. "I knew you both would come to an understanding sooner or later, that's what couples do and that's the very reason why I didn't want to join the conversation. So, when are you leaving Santy?" "Soon. As it's not an official transfer, all the time I need is just to pack my stuff."

"How are you going to deal with your manager?" Anshul asked.

"That shouldn't be a problem. WFH. They think I work from home while I work from

Hyderabad. Moreover, my manager doesn't care about those things as long as you work like an ass."

"Isn't that a good thing?"

"What is? Working like an ass?"

"Manager giving you freedom"

"Freedom to work like an ass?"

"Freedom to work from anywhere"

"Freedom to work from anywhere like an ass?"

"This is why people don't like you Santy" Utkarsh joined the conversation.

T

It's been only 2 and a half minutes but it feels like he has been there weighing half of the earth on his shoulders for the past 2 days. For him, all that mattered at that moment was to pass the next 30 seconds and hit the 3-minute mark. Time passes very slowly when you're doing a plank and time passes even slower on a Monday and if you mix both of them, like doing a plank on a Monday, there is nothing slower than the time at that moment.

Perhaps, working out is a trademark solution for all the people who suffer mentally. Though punishing your body for something that your brain did sounds so unfair, somehow it works.

He is working out for 2 strict hours daily which includes 1 hour 15 minutes of muscle training, then a 10 min break followed by 35 minutes of abs training. By the time he finishes his body is almost like a sack of sand that is punched by a set of boxers. He is dragging himself home post workouts. Those few hours made his brain so numb that he couldn't think of anything else other than getting through that period. His surroundings become immaterial and for those two hours, he fights himself and his brain stays put watching him quietly. Before this, he never knew that a physical workout can affect mental balance. He believes in it now. The body and the brain work together, but just like God, in invisible and mysterious ways.

His phone buzzed and he knew who texted him right away.

"What are you doing?" WhatsApp message.

"Working out," he replied.

"Why are you looking at the phone then?" got an instant reply.

"Priorities" he responded.

"What priorities?"

"You will understand when you prioritise someone over something."

There was no response from her for quite some time and he understood that no response is also a response and went back to his routine.

"Woah... what happened today bro?" his gym partner questioned him, "you added an extra set to every exercise" asked Rohit, his gym partner, a lean but determined guy who joined the gym a few weeks earlier to Krish. Both of them talked about their body shapes one evening during Krrish's 10-minute break and became partners after that day. They both plan each other's sets accordingly every day to balance their workout plans.

Krish couldn't tell him the actual reason but he knew that he needs to say something.

"Just increasing the dose bro, more weight on the muscles and lesser weight on the brain." Krish replied.

"Weights on the brain?" Rohit looked perplexed.

There is a gap after the question as Krish is going on with his bench press repetitions. Once he is done,

"Yeah bro, the weight of the thoughts that run in the brain."

Now, Rohit is doing his repetitions and so, couldn't say anything, and by the time they're done with the set, both forgot what they'd been talking about and just about then, Krish's phone buzzed again.

"I don't understand these priorities and all. Don't talk to me logically and don't try to make me feel guilty about how I treat you. Everyone is the same for me, there are no special priorities" the text read.

He missed the notification due to the high-volume music that's played at the gym. He noticed the text later and responded.

"So, you are saying that I'm just like everyone else you talk to." He replied.

"No, I don't talk to everyone like I talk to you." Her response came quicker than he expected.

"I'm not talking about what you talk about but the intensity or the interest with which you talk" he texted her and went back to his routine as he knew that he won't get a reply. "k" is the reply from her. 'K' as a reply is an antonym of 'okay'; It's a disgusted disapproval, opposite to an okay.

He wrote a note to himself that day which read, "Never prioritise someone to the top who doesn't even understand priorities"

20

Both of them went out for a walk to see how Independence-day is celebrated around the city.

The shop is closed for the public holiday.

"Can we just go for a walk? I feel numb sitting at home and not going out." Acharya said.

Robin wanted to say that it is just another day but he didn't and joined Acharya in the walk. He is not so keen on events and celebrations but as he agreed to accompany, he needs to swallow his discomfort.

"So, you wanted to see the celebrations around, didn't you?"

"Yeah, kind of. Laughing and joyous kids are a sight to watch."

Robin didn't approve of it. He doesn't find it very amusing; he feels that teenage girls are a sight to watch. The one who said age is just a number wouldn't have been a mathematician.

Age might just be a number but numbers are so damn important. The way we live changes with age, physically. Mentally, it changes with the ability to think and with the situations one faces.

"Boss, do you like History?"

"What?" Acharya is immersed in the surroundings.

"Do you like history?"

"Like? Who likes history? I don't think 'like' is the word. We need to learn history, remember it, and make sure it doesn't repeat. I don't think there is anything worthy enough to like, in history."

"I beg to differ, boss. Vasco de Gama discovered a way to India. The Guptas period was considered the golden age. Pyramids were constructed. There is a hell of lot of things to like, in History."

"I am sure they're all interesting but do we ever get to see the other side of the coin? Vasco discovered the way but later, he helped the Europeans invade it. The Guptas period was called a golden age by historians who only considered the scientific advances of the period but what about the differences among the people? Pyramids are sure great but do we know the name of a single person who helped lay those rocks? History is astonishing Robin. It sure is great and I appreciate it all the time but I don't like it. Great and good are two different things, I feel. I could form an opinion only if I find at least one book written by a loser of every period or every war."

Robin is not quite convinced and he said, "Let's agree to disagree."

He continued "I know I would regret this question but what makes history in your opinion?"

"The desire for forever is the fundamental stone of history." Robin replied.

Robin is standing there, without a clue.

"One makes history when one does something that lives forever. Like your example, Pyramids. But irrespective of how advanced humans get, the details are always missing. We know that Egyptians used Pyramids as tombs but we have no idea what they would have been thinking back then."

"So, you want a time machine, then?" Robin jokes.

They were done with the walk for the evening and started walking back home. Though Robin wasn't very keen on coming for a walk, he is feeling relaxed now.

"It isn't bad." Robin acknowledged.

"You don't know if you don't go," Acharya answered. "I have been thinking about what you said. I don't want a time machine."

"Just in case, if you don't know already, we don't have one even if you want it, boss." Robin tried his sarcasm.

"I want a time map, instead."

"Yeah, a new thing again. Come on, explain." Robin is hiding his curiosity behind the fun. "How wonderful would it be to have a map, not with nations but with the years on it which says which direction one needs to take at a particular point of time so that one can reach a particular destination, a map with a road called time. You see the directions of not where will you end up but how you will end up."

"But wouldn't that make lives easier? One would always know what happens if they choose a thing. The whole magic of life disappears then, I feel. I don't understand why people always fear uncertainty but I somehow believe that uncertainty is a major aspect of life that makes it interesting."

Acharya knew Robin was right. Lives would be boring if everyone knew where they would be going in time. Perhaps, this is why he loves talking to Robin. There is always room to learn a thing or two from everyone you meet and Robin doesn't care twice before expressing what he feels.

"Lots of best things happened in my life way before I understood life or love. I would have responded to a lot of things in a very different manner had they happened to me a bit later or earlier. Maybe, you're right. One needs to take a risk and perhaps, that's how one is supposed to understand life."

"Yay, I reached one of my goals," Robin shouted.

"Which is?"

"To win an argument with you, remember?"

"There isn't much of my ego left to not acknowledge your win, Robin"

"Our staff would disagree, boss."

XXI

Being understood is an underrated pleasure. All those years in Pune, Santhosh had to depend either on English or Hindi to converse. Though he never faced any problems there, now, he realizes that he missed his mother tongue. Not-needing-to-think-of-words lifts the filters before speaking. For a lot of South-Indians, secondary language doesn't come easy. Brain processes at half speed when we need to converse in any language other than the mother tongue. We need to gauge our grammar before saying anything. If you belong to that English medium sect who can speak fluent English without thinking twice, you will never understand what we go through in every client call, in every situation that involves the opposite sex. We can neither step up nor step down. Well, now, he is in full charge here. He is in a comfort zone, after all. He is sitting in a food court in the office, enjoying a fruit salad before a girl comes and stands in front of him.

"Hey, you irresponsible idiot, is this the time to come to the office?" Santhosh greeted her in their way.

"Well, no time is a good time to come to the office. Be grateful that I've come" Sravya tapped on his shoulders and both left the food court, walking towards their office building.

"So, you arranged a cubicle for me?"

"Why are you bothered about that, sit in my cube. All you need is a plugboard, isn't it?"

"Yes, I have my laptop"

"So, shut up and come."

"But I didn't say anything."

"I mean, shut your brain up and follow me. Don't think much. Looks like there wasn't anyone in Pune who could shut you up all these days."

Santhosh is thinking of Anshul, who often asked him to shut up. But he never mentioned specifically, whether the mouth or the brain that is to be shut.

It's been three days in Hyderabad Campus. Everything is so different from Pune. The people around him, the way they work, the lifestyles they have, everything. Two people who are so close to each other, who do the same job, earn the same salary, and work for the same number of hours may have two completely different lives. The person right next to you who spends the majority of the day time with you may live a lot better or a lot worse compared to you. We just don't get to know the other person completely, ever. They are a group of 5 to 6 people who go to lunch together, evening breaks, and for a walk yet no one knows what other person is going through. The beauty of human lives lies in the fact that we all look at the same thing in different ways, live the same life in different ways, and understand or misunderstand the same fact in different ways.

"We are leaving, aren't you guys coming, it's 6 pm already," the group asked Santhosh and Sravya who are still glued to their screens.

"I've installations to do man, you guys carry on" Santhosh answered. Sravya is on call and waved her hand saying, "Bye".

Two hours later both of them knew that they needed to be in the office for a long hour and so, went out of the building to grab a bite as well as to breathe some air that wasn't intoxicated with binaries.

"So, what brings you to Hyderabad?"

"I miss you people. It's been long. I haven't seen you all after college, except for you."

"I'm flattered but I would love to hear the truth"

"Why doesn't anyone trust me when I say I miss people."

"I knew you from college. Arguing with you over a lot of topics and after having several hours of discussions over our tea breaks in Pune, I think I know you better than others. So, I know you don't miss people as much as you miss places, as much as you miss experiences. And even though you miss some people, I'm sure that missing people wouldn't impact you enough to change your job location."

"That's not true. I do miss people and that does make me take strong decisions but…." Sravya interrupted, 'I've been waiting for this 'but' Santhosh smiled. "But that may not be the reason this time. I am so bored with what I'm doing right now. I have been surrounded by the same people for years now, working under and working with them. These things aren't giving me anything new to ponder about. Worrying about the same thing doesn't help me move forward. I need to find new problems, need to find new circumstances to deal with."

"How moving here is going to help those purposes?"

"I'm yet to find that but at least the people I'm surrounded with have changed. The food, and the problems of the place change for starters. I've to travel to Rwanda for my next assignment in a few days. So, till then, this place would get me excited."

"So, we are all guinea pigs to you, just the case studies."

"If that's the case, I could have gone to the any of the campuses but chose this one to have you guys around."

"Fair point. Finish your corn and let's get back to work."

u

Time froze for their relationship as it is not going anywhere but relatively, it's moving. It's moving faster than usual. It's already 8 months into their course and the college fest is going to be organised soon. Soon after that, they'll have their departmental farewell and other formalities of finishing the academic year. Their second semester exams are due in another 2 months. We never discussed their first semester because it didn't matter. They both passed the semester and that is all there to it. Krish and Prags are sitting in the classroom during the lunch hour like they used to do all the time. The surroundings are the same but they are not, anymore. They are not the same people they were a few months ago. They are sitting next to each other, with her hand resting on his shoulder yet they are farther than they were when he left for Sri Lanka. Sometimes, we are so close to the people who are millions of miles away but at times, we are very far from a person who is sitting right next to us. Isn't it all about how strong the bond is, irrespective of the distance between the two people? This question never gives a concrete answer.

"How many days is the fest going to be?" Prags is curious.

"No idea" he replied without looking up from the book he was reading.

"Any idea about what all will part of it?" she continues.

"No. I don't know. I feel they're boring" he confessed.

"Okay, irrespective of how you like it, I'm going to attend it. The first fest of my student life" She is excited.

That statement irked him. Irrespective of his opinion or presence, she is going to attend it anyway. He decided not to attend the fest right then and there, if not for anything, just to test how much she meant it.

"I'm not going to attend," he replied.

"What? Why?" she is surprised, takes her hand off his shoulder, and says "Why won't you attend the fest? Where are you going?"

"As if it matters," he murmured.

"What?" she asked as she couldn't quite hear what he said.

"I'm visiting my friend's place. I have a cricket match to be part of" he made up a reason.

Yes, there is a cricket match and yes, he is required in the team but he never thought about it till then.

"Oh, ok" Prags is disappointed. "Whom should I roam around with?"

"You planned to attend it irrespective of my presence, so, you will figure out a way" he is cold in his responses.

"Yeah," she answered.

He is still looking down at the book but no words are being read, no lines are passed, no pages are turned. He is stuck there again because of his foolishness of dragging the discussion too far. She wanted him to be there, with her, all the time, but he spoilt it. Time froze again, for him. It's freezing too often these days with the mind resisting to move ahead of the situation. He is unable to bear the fact that every person can have individual choices to make. Doesn't matter whether you are in a relationship or not, you can make choices that do not affect the other person directly. He shouldn't have tried to rub his opinion of fests on her and when he did, he should've been ready to accept the disagreement.

He left for the cricket match the same night and still hoped for her not to attend the fest without him. He was about to text her the next morning to confirm but by then, he saw a WhatsApp status with her and his other classmates attending an event. There wasn't much that he could do and he focussed on what was at hand and scored a century in the match. He seems to be more productive when he's sad. His workouts proved that and now, his game stats too.

21

"Woah! Wrong delivery?" Robin asked.

"Nope," Acharya said.

"These flowers and greeting cards are delivered for us?"

"Yes."

"For what?"

"It's the shop's anniversary. My friends must have sent these."

"You remember dates like that? And you've friends? And they remember dates like that?" Robin started shelling.

"Ha-ha"

The worst thing that can ever happen to someone who asks a set of questions is to be smiled at. Robin is disappointed and furious but can't express either.

"Where are our employees? None of them are here yet?"

"I am repeating the anniversary activities. They're all on holiday."

"What do you mean by repeating the activities?"

"It was only me when I opened the shop so, it would be only me today. This gets repeated every year."

"Is this how you celebrate? I thought there would be some kind of party."

"Well, this is. On a birthday, they give you birthday bumps so that you cry, repeating what you did when you were born, on an anniversary, I'm working alone which I did the first time."

"So, on a marriage day, do I need to remarry?"

"You just need to re-promise everything you promised her." Acharya took a break. "Yes, I've friends, who are old now. They couldn't visit the shop on anniversaries anymore but they sent flowers. But I can assure you that they will visit if something happens to me. So, I've them to defend me."

"Good for you."

"Who do you have?"

"What?"

"Whom do you have in your defence?"

"Philosophy."

"Sarcasm is my sword; Philosophy is my shield," Acharya said in a deeper voice. "Ever heard that?"

"That's a nice one, I am wondering why I never heard of that."

"You liked that because it was written by someone your age and you never heard of it because it was written by me."

"When you were young?"

"Yes, When I was your age. I used sarcasm to beat people and philosophy to defend them. At least, I thought so. I thought I was immune to feelings and emotions."

"Another explanation coming?"

"Experience coming."

"Please go on."

"I thought I was wise to use Philosophy but then later when I sat down understanding, I realised that I used philosophy only to escape. Escaping reality is a pleasure and that could come in any way. For me, it was philosophy. Used it all the time to duck the situations which were supposed to be handled by me. I used it as a shield but I never moved forward. I just stood my ground and defended everything that came my way. Philosophy teaches us to do a lot of things and also not to do a few. I only focussed on the things that philosophy taught me not to do."

"So, what do you feel now?"

"All philosophy and reason are the aftermath of emotions."

"Please explain."

"Going back to the old ages, Neo Frontal Cortex was developed so much later, only after humans started thinking and they started thinking only when they felt something. For example, Primal emotion like fear made humans find a cave, they used reason to find one but the root was fear, an emotion."

"Do you have scientific proof for your statements?"

"My above explanation is an emotion, don't go reasoning."

XXII

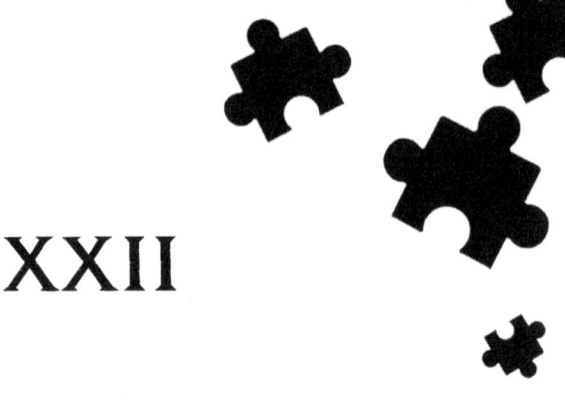

Santhosh landed in Kigali, the capital of Rwanda where he needs to work for the next 3 months. The journey of over 10km from the Kigali International Airport to the centre of the city is uphill. On reaching the place, he realised it was kind of a hill station. At an elevation of 1567 metres (above sea level), Kigali is the economic and cultural hub of the nation. The city looked peaceful and well built. For a nation that faced genocide less than 20 years ago, the way they lifted themselves and the process of progression is impressive. Post-genocide, the responsibility and the burden of the development were left to the women as most of the men from the families were killed. In response, Rwandan women did a great job lifting the nation and making it one of the top five most developed countries since 2000. In 20 years, Rwanda became one of the safest countries to live in. Kigali, the capital city of Rwanda is the cleanest city in Africa. Rwanda is the second-best African country to do business in, only second to Mauritius. We can see what those women did to the nation right in front of our eyes. Rwanda boasts a record of female representatives in their parliament with over 60%. He read and realised all these the very day he reached Kigali. In the process, he wondered whether the men all around are making the world a bit more complicated. How different the world would have been, had it been handled by the ladies?

****

The work is the same, as what he has been doing for the past 4 years. The client, the people he works with, the surroundings, and the places are changing but the work is more or less, the same. He is waiting for the weekends just so that he can explore Rwanda. That's the reason he has been accepting the onsite offers, to visit new places. Well, he would be lying if he says money doesn't matter, it does but more than that, it's the travelling that he is inclined to. He is using his profession just to feed his passion. So, on-site assignments are like double shots.

He gets to travel and partially, it's been paid by the organisation. The price for all this is the boring work that he needs to do during the week. But more often than not, he ponders, is it worth to sacrifice the whole week for the weekend and feel disgusted on a Monday morning.

Saturdays are for the trips; Sunday mornings are mostly lost in sleep and Sunday nights are for the drinks. These are the agreed terms of the plan for the 3 months that he is going to stay there. They have planned for the famous Gorilla Trek in Rwanda, the rare adventure that you get to do only in Uganda, Rwanda, and DR Congo. In Congo, you get to see the lowland gorillas whereas, in Uganda and Rwanda, it's the mountain Gorillas. These adventures are open throughout the year but the best time to visit is in July, August, and November as there won't be heavy rains which help the treks. It costs $1500 per head per trip and you get to spend an hour with the Gorillas. People are taken in groups of 8 and only 10 groups are allowed per day as the authorities don't want their habitat to be affected. We are not allowed to touch or go near them as they share over 98% of our DNA and are capable of catching Flu and other diseases from humans. There are several reasons for the high cost of the adventure as 75% of it goes to the conservation of the gorillas, 10% goes to the local communities around the park and the rest is bagged by the government. Along with the gorilla trek, they wanted to cover a hot spring (there are 5 volcanoes in Rwanda) and Lake Kivu.

That night after coming back from a day full of adventures, he goes through his gallery to see which one to upload to his social platforms. After posting one, he started thinking. There is always this phase, post-dinner, and pre-slumber, that's the toughest phase of the day. The time when the heart starts thinking, and questioning, to which the brain seldom finds answers. He spent an hour sitting with the gorillas that were so calm, walking, eating, hugging rangers, and laughing at them while the whole gang of 8 people around them were busy clicking photos. We all need to re-learn a lot of things from animals. Enjoying the present is for one. His heart started asking him questions.

Heart: Is this what you're intending to do for the rest of your life? Suffer a week to live a day?

Brain: Lots of people aren't even living, we get to live at least a day.

Heart: You're wrong, lots of people are living the lives they wanted, cherishing every minute. We are getting to live only a day.

Brain: Those are the minority.

Heart: From when the minorities are irrelevant?

Brain: What do you want me to do? To quit the job?

Heart: Oh, that's your job, think it out. All I can say is that I'm not 100% liking it. If you care for me, you know what you need to do. Just to remind you, I'm a guy who is complete only with art. HE feels complete only with ART.

He + Art = Heart.

Brain: Don't bring in the name game, the names are in your favour. I can't dissect mine. It involves a bra.

A lot more discussions happen inside his head almost every day, to be specific, every night. If you're not happy before going to sleep, you're not happy with your life. The struggles in the outside world are nothing compared to his internal battles. They don't settle down ever, they don't stop talking. He is a prisoner of his thoughts. As great as it is called, evolution couldn't get humans a brain that can feel and a heart that can think. While the heart is like Champagne which is very eager to spill all its emotions out of the bottle, the conscience is the cork that's controlling it. This internal war is endless and doesn't stop unless you submit yourself to your passion. Only on that day do the brain and heart agree, and agree upon what to do further, together.

V

He came back to the hostel on the last day of the fest after it ended and she left for home.

They didn't talk for 3 days, the whole time while he was away, while the fest happened. Unknowingly, both of them are helping the gaps between them to increase. They met in the classroom after 5 days as the fest ended on a Friday evening.

"So, are you staying for the farewell or do you have a game to play?" she asked him. Those were the first lines that she spoke to him, after 5 days, clearly explaining that she wasn't done with that yet.

"Don't know for sure yet" he is always up for an argument.

"Go, you might be needed very much there, more than here" sarcasm isn't her field of expertise but she nailed it here.

"Visibly," he said.

The farewell day arrived. He explained that he would be in the campus but wouldn't be attending the farewell as she would again be talking to the senior and he wouldn't be able to bear it. He made it clear that it would hurt him so much. Her response to all his explanations was unclear and didn't clarify anything. So, while the classrooms are getting decorated for the function, he is in the library reading about a Chinese Soup in the Travel and Leisure magazine. She didn't bother much and is participating in the classroom programs. Krish has the complete schedule for the program. He planned to attend the program an hour late when the speeches start so that he could avoid any pre-program activities where she indulges in moving close to her peers. So, he gave it another 10-minute grace period and went to the department. Just when he turned left towards his class room he saw her dancing with the senior there, giggling. For a moment, he didn't know what to do. Stopped, turned back, and then, turned around, and headed straight to the washroom and she saw him just about then.

"Thanks for coming, I was bored" she is quick to acknowledge his presence.

"Oh, but it didn't seem that way. You seem to be having some wonderful time" he is furious but doesn't have a reason behind it. First thing after entering the washroom, he questioned his own integrity. When he decided not to come, why did he and these are the leisure activities, how could he trust the schedule? How did he expect things to take place on time? All these questions made him look like a fool and he probably is furious at himself but as there is no way to express it to himself, he is dishing it out on her.

"Why are you angry?" She is clueless.

"You didn't seem to have the faintest of sadness about me not being here. You don't miss me, do you?" he is asking questions before she can answer. "How could you enjoy when I'm not here, when I'm sitting somewhere miserably?" Along with water, he seemed to have flushed his maturity in the washroom. It was his own choice to sit somewhere miserable and is now pushing it onto her.

"See, these are not daily things that are happening here. Farewell is a once-a-year activity and just because you don't want to be part of it doesn't mean that everyone needs to boycott it.

Neither did I force you to come nor did I stop you from coming. It was your choice and now, why are you blaming me?" she sounded so mature, didn't sound like someone he had known for all those months. He knew what she said was right but still believed that as a couple, one does hold the key to the partner's happiness and he wanted her to be more responsible in handling his feelings. But he didn't have any answers to shoot back with. He waited till the whole program ended.

After the program ended, they are waiting at their spot again. It's been so many days since they sat there because of her dancing classes and his workouts. Both used to leave right after class without any time for themselves, alone. They're not going to meet for quite some time, 2 weeks to be specific as they're given the preparation holidays for the semester.

"So, on the exam day again?" he asked her.

"Mostly, unless they call us for the hall ticket someday in between" she responded with a smirk.

"Okay then, I'll not be in the hostel, will come back a day or two before the exam." He said.

"Oh okay" she has nothing more to say, "Let's meet then. Bye" she started moving towards the bus.

"Prags" he called her, "Love you". It sounded so sad but his sincerity is visible.

She smiled and left.

22

"What happened to the Robin who went out?" Acharya stopped Robin on his way back into the shop.

"Excuse me??"

"The other Robin, peaceful one."

"Oh! He suffered an intense discussion and peaceful Robin is now pieces of Robin."

"Srishti again?"

"Who else do you think would have power to turn me into a monster?"

"Well, what happened?"

"She disappoints me in some or another way. It is like she is doing a thesis on how to disappoint me."

"Well, with a great girlfriend comes great disappointments."

"Why are relationships always associated with pain? Why is suffering always a part of love?"

"Because pain and pleasure are just two sides of the same coin but we don't concentrate enough to look at both sides together."

"But is it worth it?"

"That's the problem, Robin. We try to generalise a lot of things that are not supposed to be generalized. It is an individual choice, there should never be a question of whether it is worth it or not. For you, it might, and for someone else, it might not."

"But how will we ever know who is worthy enough to cause us pain?"

"You got a dog, he doesn't care about whether you are worthy of his love or not, he just decides that you're and in time, you become one. Similarly, someday you will be with someone and you will decide."

"But how will we know whether they are the ones or not?"

"We don't have tails to wag Robin, it's eyes for humans."

"Maybe but I must admit that I always feel the road of love is very bumpy."

"Says a guy who likes adventures." Acharya never misses a chance to give it back.

"Yeah, make fun of me. What do you know? Single old man. I doubt whether you ever loved someone and even if you did, she would have left you because you have answers for all these situations, the self-made solutions which you use."

Acharya went mute, Robin looked guilty.

"Everything you did in years can be flushed off by what you say in two seconds. So, be careful with the words Robin."

Robin seemed genuinely guilty "I am sorry, boss. I wasn't in the right frame of mind." Robin is frustrated at himself for letting the anger get the better of him.

"Hmm. Go home today. Take a leave from the shop as well as your room. Come, join us tomorrow." Acharya said. Robin didn't say a word understanding that it was not a statement but an order.

****

Robin is not someone who would visit home often, he likes to stay away from it, from all the emotional baggage the home carries. He felt guilty after what he said to his boss and he did apologise but that didn't help the situation. He is now sitting under a tree in a public park thinking about what he could have done, rather than what he shouldn't have done. "It is true, what you say can change what you did, in all the years," Robin told himself. He got up and decided to meet his boss at home to apologise again. He felt that he was not capable of persuasive apologies but he didn't want to leave any stone unturned.

XXIII

"So, have you missed me for the last 3 months?" Santhosh wanted to say these words right after entering his cubicle but it didn't work out as he was so early in the office, at 10:30 am, Sravya walked in 15 minutes later.

"You, unprofessional employees, coming so late to the office" Santhosh murmured.

"I didn't hear that there are any vacancies in the HR team," Sravya responded.

"Why is that a problem now?"

"Because you're behaving like one. Why are you bothered with my office timings?"

He didn't have a genuine answer except for his wrong expectation so he kept quiet.

"And aren't you supposed to be back 15 days ago? You said it was only for 3 months, you got it extended for 15 days?"

"Nah, I went on a trip"

"What? Where? When?"

"I visited several parts of the seven sisters, North East India"

"For 15 days?"

"Yeah, for 15 days, all by myself, alone again."

"We, being your friends, don't feel that you work enough, being on trips all the time and relaxing the rest of the time, I wonder how your manager is taking it up and how did he approve your 2-week leaves for the trip."

"Oh, he didn't. I went for it anyway"

"Did he take it well?"

"He would have, maybe, had I not put my papers"

"Are you crazy, you resigned because he didn't grant you leave?"

Santhosh discussed this with his manager and that resulted in the below self-conversation. He recollected the whole incident and also the meeting that happened inside his head.

Brain: I'm tired of dealing with all these, every day. You take over for one day and do whatever you want.

Heart: This is the moment I've been waiting for all my life.

Brain: What are you planning to do?

Heart: None of your business, for today.

Brain: I need to face the consequences of whatever you do today.

Heart: If you can't even take that simple responsibility, what's the point in being called the "most important organ of a human body."

Brain: Don't bring that conversation up again, it's always been in debates about the "most important organ". Lots of people still support you while it's clear that you're such a stupid.

Heart: Let's see who will look stupid from tomorrow.

"Come on, open your mouth" Sravya stressed again.

"It's not exactly for that reason. I have been longing to do something different from this Sravs, I've been thinking of this for some time now. It took me three overseas assignments and these many years to realise that I love travelling more than anything."

"So, you resigned? You can travel while working as well, right."

"I can but I realised that's not what I wanted. I can't work for 5 days just so that I could feel alive for 2 days."

"This sounds so stupid to me, but that's okay, when did you sound normal anyway" Sravya sighed.

Sravya knew there was more to it than what he was saying. She wanted to know more, to understand his actual intentions behind the move. Both of them went for a break in the evening just like every day, post-tea but with no one else accompanying them today. She knew he would push it away if there were people who wouldn't take him seriously, who wouldn't understand what he means when he says something. If he feels that one can't fathom what he says, he doesn't like to trouble them with his depth. She knew it and so, she wanted to talk to him in his most vulnerable state, the state when he feels that he is most safe, alone. We all want to see or talk to people in their vulnerable phases, probably because that's when people reveal their true selves.

"This life is mundane; I don't even want to talk about it" Sravya initiated a conversation while they are walking back to the office from the food court.

"That's the problem with all of us, we don't address the things that we need to. Our lives are indeed mundane and we aren't even talking about it. I don't understand why no one stresses much about it. Why does everyone think that getting a job is the ultimate salvation?"

Santhosh sounded calmer than normal. Especially while talking about stuff like this, about life, he suddenly becomes so intense and conscious that he doesn't take many jokes about it. Even if he does, he comes up with a philosophical explanation for everything, but not this time. He looked so relaxed.

"Is that why you are quitting?"

"I don't have one particular reason behind this move, Sravs. It's the result of an accumulation of emotions over the years.

The mid-twenties are a great learning period for boys. To be precise, around 24 to 27.

Stuck between two thoughts. Should we take risks and chase what we always wanted to do or be like everyone else, do our jobs, support our family, and then raise our own? Unable to decide whether to chase their dreams and take the road less travelled, or get into the routine. Among these circumstances, you get to meet kids and you think you are going to have a nice time, that lasts only until someone calls you uncle. You may ask what's wrong with that, but the way kids address you reminds you that you don't have much time left to choose the path, to decide the further steps of your life. Girlfriend (you can't call her ex because you still love her) gets married but by mid-twenties, you understand what love is and you can't move on and love someone just like that. You may try but at a point, you realise that no one is like her and it's unfair to compare but you can't always win the battle with your brain. The heart is a weak warrior when it comes to the war of logic. Living with the memories is the only option that will be left. You neither want to be single nor want to get married. Choosing a career suddenly becomes so difficult. You feel like losing everything you liked, every loss becomes a lesson you don't want to learn. Stuck with the same cubicle and keyboard while the heart longs for something new but the brain drags you back and hits your face right on the solid rocks of reality. Your friends and peers start getting married and they look happy, at least on social media. Some are single and others are committed but everyone else looks happy while you find yourself on the other side of the world. As a part of society, you start wearing the fake-smile mask all the time. After a while, we even forget that we're wearing masks, we forget our true faces. We become the masks.

With your job, parents think that you're an achiever but you realise that you're stuck in the endless loop of obeying orders and feeling suppressed. Every day, a new question hits you while you're still searching for the answers to the questions that were posed a week ago. You start owning every meme posted on social sites. Among all these questions, we learn about life. We realise that some things are not meant to be controlled. We learn how to cope. We learn how to kill dreams, and how to smile through tears. As someone said, the graveyard is one of the most valuable places ever. There are a lot of unexplained thoughts, unaccomplished dreams, unpursued paths, unfinished goals, and also unexpressed love we take along with us.

I am at a juxtaposition; I just don't know what to do. This hasn't happened to me so far because I have been just following the procedure laid out by our seniors, just doing what everyone else was doing. Once I decided to do something different, all of a sudden, I was left with a lot of questions to answer. But I guess it's worth it. For now, I only know that this is not what I want to do, so I decided to quit but anyway, I've three months of notice period to serve now."

"So, do you have any plans of re-thinking the resignation?"

"Oh no, that's finalised. No backstepping from that. I want to enjoy these last 3 months of my first job. And you have done well to get all this information from me. I must admit you have done well, starting the discussion and bringing life into it. I've been longing to talk to someone about this. Thank you"

"No, I didn't mean to probe in but I knew you've something more to say. I thought it may ease you off a bit if you share."

"Thank you. Everyone has a story to tell but they don't often find people who is ready to listen. How often do you find a person who would just listen without judging. Thanks for listening."

"Don't start with it again very early in the morning. That's my display picture and I won't change it" text read. He texted her in the morning two days after their last meeting and asked her to change her WhatsApp display picture as he felt it is revealing.

"It's above the knees. Come on, thighs are visible. Change it to something else" he replied.

"That's a skirt and that's how it will be. And what rights do you think you have to ask me to change it?"

"What? A boyfriend doesn't have a right over it?"

"You are not my boyfriend and boyfriends have a choice of expressing their opinions but not rights of deciding what their girlfriends get to wear."

He is perplexed by the reply, especially the first part of it.

"I am not your boyfriend?" he still can't believe it.

"No, you are not"

"We broke up? When did that happen?" The conversation is still happening over the texts.

"I told you a lot of times that you're hindering my freedom. In a lot of ways, on a lot of days, you broke me, literally. I went to sleep crying many times just because of your restrictions."

"Can I call you?" His text interrupted her long essays.

"No, I don't want to talk. Don't call me. You misunderstood a lot of things and misinterpreted the rest. You never gave me a chance to explain. You were so harsh on me. I didn't even have the freedom to talk to other people casually. I stopped going to the dance classes just to spend more time with you and you ruined it. All the extra minutes I spent with you, you put extra effort into hurting me in one way or the other. I don't want to go through all that anymore. I want to be free. I don't want to force myself to think before doing anything and I am not blaming you for everything. I may have made mistakes from my side too. We are not meant to be and it's better if you understand that both of us should part ways."

He is numb. His fingers aren't moving. Well, even if they did, he didn't know what to type. He still can't fathom that it is over. He put the phone aside, got up, folded his blanket, and made up the bed, re-reading all those messages in his head. Everything else around him is happening subconsciously. After a few minutes passed (no one knows how many) he picked up the phone to respond to her but by then, there were a few more texts lined up for him.

"I know both of us are on the faulty side, we both made mistakes and none of us are willing to mend them. So, it's always better to get out of the gates when there is still a small passage available. I don't want us to move forward and get all tangled in the uncomfortable situations again."

He is shocked to see the maturity in those texts.

"You said that you didn't want to think before doing anything but all these texts seem to be well-thought." Out of all that he wanted to say, this was the first response from him. Yeah, face-palm moment.

"I think before making important decisions" she is straight to the point.

"I know I made you very uncomfortable, quite a few times by being restrictive and forcing rules but that was all done because of my immense possessiveness. I thought that you understood. It was my mistake to assume that you understood those situations. They weren't normal and I should have explained them to you. How about both of us sit and decide on what factors both of us will compromise on? How about you name your top priorities into which I won't get my nose in and vice versa."

"No. I don't want to take this any further. I don't want to compromise on anything, that is the whole reason behind this. And I don't trust you anymore. Today, you may say that you won't poke into those things but soon enough, even before knowing, you will be there, pinching about the same old things. This won't work out. Understand that once it reaches a state like this, it'll never be the same again. It would only be an amended relationship which won't be pure anymore."

While he sounded mature all this time and she was a kid, these are the inverse times. She is making sense with every other line she is saying and he is just there with unreliable hope that he has. He is still trying to hang on to the branch that has already fallen off the tree. She is done with it and is not in the mood to even think about it any further.

But for him, this hit harder than anything that he ever faced before. Not the fact of them breaking up but the time when it happened, when he least expected it coming. He too knew that the bond wasn't as cemented as it used to be or as he wanted it to be but was never expecting her to call it off. The news of her ending it shocked him more than the fact that it ended. Perhaps, the male ego is acting on him even without him knowing it.

"Okay. I should have seen the signs earlier. It is my mistake to not detect the varying patterns. From your side, you gave me enough signs but I never even had this thought of moving away so, couldn't think in that direction. All the best for your future endeavours. I don't think I'm allowed to say anything else. For one last time, I love you." He texted her back. He claims to be the one who hung on to it. Yes, the message sounds deep and heavy but we can never be sure of its authenticity, how much he actually meant of what he said. There are few things that we can never measure or gauge and there is always uncertainty about the amount of truth. More often than not, it's love that causes these kinds of situations.

"I love you too but I don't want us to go ahead" she replied.

For once, she is behaving maturely as he always wanted her to be. For once, she is thinking before doing anything and he is hating it. He never thought that his advice would work against him.

23

"Did you forget the rules?" Acharya shouted.

Robin went in without knocking on his door. He forgot the rules. We tend to make mistakes when we feel emotional and it all falls apart especially when we try to mend something, when we try to repair it. Robin is gutted.

"I'm sorry boss. I came to apologise for what I said earlier and now, I don't know which one I should apologise first for." He sounded sad.

Robin enters the room for the first time and he is surprised to look at everything that is around. He never imagined the room to be so occupied. It is so dark but he could see that it is full of books, gift-wrapped items, photographs, and sticky notes pasted all over the walls. He knew that he is not allowed to peek but he couldn't help and Acharya isn't stopping him.

"I'm sorry boss."

"You said that already, sit down."

"Am I allowed to…" Robin was about to ask but he refrained himself. The best thing that you could do, at times, is to keep your mouth shut. Robin did understand that for once.

"Today is the 11th of May."

"Yes sir."

"It's the Anniversary of Memories."

"The store?"

"Store too was opened on the same day." Acharya is holding a card "Yes, you were right. I did love someone and she did leave me."

"Boss, I'm sorry, I didn't mean it."

"No, Robin, we both know you meant it and that is true."

"Boss, Can I switch on the lights? I can't see a thing."

"That's how dark it is in my head, Robin. It's a symbolic reference, don't spoil it. And, I thought you like darkness."

"I do."

"More often than not, we figure out life in the dark instead of in the lights."

"Yes, boss." Robin seems to have gone into a yes-sir mode like they do in the forces, irrespective of what is told to them.

"I account for the sin of burning down someone's memories Robin. I had a friend who had a failed relationship and was getting married. She asked me to burn down all their physical memories, photos, letters, and stuff. I wanted to read all those letters before burning them, at the least to understand what the guy would have felt but I couldn't break the trust of my friend. She trusted me to burn them to ashes and that's what I did. Even as a third person, that didn't make me feel good, the memories turning into ashes. But there was nothing I could do. Every year, I start my anniversary with that memory. Ironic, Isn't it? To celebrate an anniversary of memories memorising a memory burning down memories."

Robin has never seen this side of his boss. Acharya is not his usual self, not even close. He is walking down the lane of maze named memories and that doesn't seem to have either a happy road or a happy destination.

"Generations have changed, huh! We used to write letters and when one breaks up, they had to burn down the letters. It wasn't easy for someone to see the words written for them getting squished, to see a letter written only for you in their own hand-writing getting burnt. But now, we forget everything just by deleting a text."

"There are always ways to suffer, boss. Even now, we have screenshots, chat exports to go

back in time."

"Hmm." Acharya knew he is right.

"Boss?"

"Yes"

"About the girl who left you…"

"Yeah?"

"Do you want to talk about it? What happened?" Robin is curious but he tries to make it sound as concerning as he could.

Acharya almost broke into tears. The human body is a strange thing. when something is burning, it generally results in a fire but for humans, it's the opposite, results in water, tears!

XXIV

"No Dhiraj, 5 pm is my swimming time, I can't attend any calls after 5" Santhosh is on the phone talking to his manager. "Nope, I'll be at the office between 9 to 5 and I feel, a phone is a personal thing and I keep my professional and personal life separate so, I don't entertain calls from work on my mobile. Drop a mail and I'll attend during the office hours."

"Yeah, we can have a Skype call, again only during office hours" he dropped the call and started giggling.

"Who was that on the phone?" Sravya wanted to know.

"My Project Manager"

"Is that how you talk to your PM?" she is surprised.

"I used to talk a little better earlier but now, I'm leaving the organisation in a few days. It's the payback time. The way they ignored me; they need to get the taste of their own medicine."

"But don't you think it's wrong?"

"Come on Sravs, no one's doing any social service here, everyone works for their salary. Your Project Manager is just another employee, superior by position in the organisation but that doesn't make you their slave."

"But, did you do this earlier?"

"Oh yeah, a lot of times. No one from my team calls me without texting me first. Even my lead. The team lead pings me first to say that he may call me at so and so time. I'm not a part of any workgroups on WhatsApp and have never been. They all may talk about me in several ways behind my back. Well, I don't care."

"I don't think a lot of people would approve of following this but I'm sure most of them would like to do the same. Not having to think about work after 5 in the evening is more relaxing than a beer on a weekend. But I should admit that I can't do this, most of us can't afford to do this."

"That's the story you tell yourself Sravs, you can do it and almost everyone can do it."

"Let's see. By the way, when is your last working day here?"

"Tomorrow."

"What?"

"Yeah, I need to go back to Pune to submit all the company's assets. That's my base location, remember? I'm not here on an official transfer. And anyway, I want to visit the Pune campus too. I am leaving tomorrow night for Pune. I've 2 days, will be able to meet everyone I know there."

"I wanted to ask, what's your next plan but refrained because I know what you'll say" Santhosh smiled while sipping his coffee.

X

"So, tell me where are we going? Any particular place in mind or just a random journey?"

Pradeep asked Krish.

After the discussion Krish had with Prags, he couldn't think of anything for a day and the only one who came to his mind was his friend, who is currently in Mumbai. A friend from college who lived with him during their college days is now working in Mumbai. He packed a couple of dresses and moved there, without a second thought. He didn't have much options too.

"Lonavala, Lavasa, Mahabaleshwar, Dapoli, Goa… where are we going? Come on" Pradeep knew how much Krish is inclined towards travel and is expecting Krish to visit him to go places together.

Krish didn't say a word. He is quiet and Pradeep smelled something wrong. He asked him, "What's wrong mama?". Pradeep is genuinely concerned now.

There is still no response. Pradeep has kept his laptop aside; he was googling all the nearby places that can be covered. Now, he is sure that something is off which is bothering Krish. He also knew he is one of the 2 or 3 people that Krish can open up to. So, he realised he has something to crack.

"What happened, mama? I'm here to listen and you know, I won't judge"

"What happens? The same story, different time, different place, and different person" Krish replied.

"Being a bit specific might help mama. Don't talk riddles." Pradeep smiled at him. There is this unique and special ability that friendship holds, exclusively. You can be sarcastic or make fun of someone who is suffering and the other person won't take it to heart. Please remember that happens only among friends. Never try that anywhere else. Not with your girlfriend or relatives or worse, your superiors at work.

"The same thing happened mama, which happens to a lot of people. I'm one of the everyone now, just another guy with a broken heart." Krish replied staring at his mobile.

"What are you looking at? Your photos together?" Pradeep asked him.

"No. I'm just looking at the blank screen. But thanks for reminding me; I need to delete all those photos. I can't believe that there is no 'US' anymore."

"So, how did it happen?"

"The same way it always happens. I fell in love and then sank into it."

Pradeep realised that this is going to be a long discussion and he is a little upset that they are not going on a trip but that is not one of the problems he is going to have now. He is unaware of how Krish would behave after something like this. Pradeep has no prior experience with these kind of scenarios and it's not an exaggeration to say that he is a little worried about what is waiting for him in the store.

"But why, what did she say? assuming she is a she. I mean I've no idea about anything at all. I didn't even know that you were… are in love. But how did she end it? I mean why did she end it?" Pradeep is clueless about what he should ask.

Krish stared at him blankly for a second or two. In a discussion, a second or two feels long, very long. Pradeep waited.

"It's like a dialogue in one of those movies. She said that a bitter ending is better than an endless bitterness and asked me to understand it."

"Wow, that's a beautiful line. Which movie is it from?" Pradeep's curiosity is genuine.

Krish is not in the mood to catch that. He is lying down and staring at the ceiling blatantly.

"What are you planning to do or what do you want to do Krish?"

"I sank so deep in it and it's so dark in here. I have no idea how to go ahead. I'm so deep in it that if I start moving up, it takes years for me to swim up and see the sunshine but then, I will be at the same place. Another way is to just start moving ahead in the dark instead of trying to get out of this. What should I do?"

Pradeep isn't sure whether that is a question or just an expression. He is confused between the options of advising him or just staying quiet and waiting until he starts talking again. He decided to provide his two cents.

"How about you move diagonally in the upward direction so that you move up and also move ahead simultaneously?" he advised.

"You were a mechanical engineering student, weren't you?" Krish asked him which he already knew for sure.

"Of course."

"See, this is what the four years of mathematics classes do to you and this is one of the reasons why you're and will forever be single." Krish could manage a smile.

"Still better than being in a relationship and suffering." He shot back instantly.

"That's true though." Krish agreed.

"But why did she feel so suffocated? What did you do so bad that she had to break the relationship to feel free?"

"Love is a bond and what does a bond do? It binds. But she wants to be completely free like a single bird flying with the wings wide open towards an undetermined goal."

"So, you feel that everyone in love needs to compromise?"

"What do you feel?"

"Who am I, a single guy, for life? What do I know?"

"I feel that sooner or later, both have to adjust or compromise on a few things to keep it alive."

"But I think I know a lot of people who are happy without making any changes to their life styles or habits."

"Are they? Are you sure they're happy or are you sure that they didn't change anything about themselves?"

24

"I thought she was the light in the dark, did not realise that she was the fire that came to consume." Acharya went quite for a minute and resumed, "We always realise a lot of things very late. There is always a line that one should never cross but we see the line only after crossing it, the line of losing self. But I can't blame her, she was the one who brought that happiness into my life and it was again her who took it back along with her."

"Why aren't we ever content with ourselves? Who invented these necessities like finding a soulmate or a better half and stuff? Whosoever it is, they didn't understand or experience the beauty of solitude. Boss, it is so beautiful. Just like a deep valley, Solitude is scary and beautiful at the same time. It is difficult to survive the fall but once you do, it is addictive."

"We are content and complete with ourselves Robin, but when someone enters our life, they introduce a new version of ourselves to us and when they leave, we miss that version of ourselves and that makes us feel incomplete. We show a different side of us to every other person, it's almost like we are a different self with every person and when one of them leaves, we lose one of those personalities, and that hurts a lot, not to be able to live one of your personalities. So, it is debatable whether a person can fill any void inside us but for sure, every person is capable of leaving one. That is why few people are scared to fall in love."

It was intended for Robin and he knew it. "Yes boss, it's true that I am… that a lot of people are scared to fall in love. That is because when you give yourself away and let the other person take a piece of you but you get nothing in return, that's when you close the doors, you start building the walls, and you stop people from approaching. They approach and then, they poach."

"We all construct the concrete walls of assumptions and start guarding them. You need to guard the walls only as long as you've them, Robin. Break them and it will all be better."

"Not easy, boss."

"Who said it's going to be easy? Anything worth doing isn't easy."

"Boss, coming back to you, do you hate that girl?"

"I do. I hate her, I hate her a lot but I just can't stop loving her. All those memories are like roses grown inside the garden of the heart. Beautiful to remember but the thorns keep hurting."

"I feel you, boss."

"Do you? Really?"

"Yes, I do."

"Just have the courage to repeat these exact words in a church, someday." Acharya never fails to use a situation.

"That is a different dimension." Robin is happy to have the mood changed. "Boss, I am going to switch on the lights."

"Okay."

Robin switched on the lights and to his surprise, all the images around that room are portraits of his boss. But every one of them is from a different location. It mesmerised Robin to realise how much Acharya would have travelled.

"Have you been to all these places?" Robin is still observing the photos.

"Yes."

"All of these. You've covered all states of the nation."

"Yeah, every state in every season, except for Rajasthan in Summer. I was too scared to visit Rajasthan in Summer but I regret that now. As someone said, we often regret the things we didn't more than the things we did."

"How did you manage to cover all these? It is amazing to have been part of every corner of the country. I always dream of it."

"Everything comes at a cost, Robin but we don't always get to see the price tag. I had to lose something or the other to have those experiences. Every single time, there was a cost. I even lost a few people."

"You lost people, too?"

"Yes."

"How did you bear that? I mean, didn't that feel terrible?"

"It does but sometimes, it's okay to be the villain of your own story."

"Okay. But how are you sitting at the same corner table every day now, for years? For someone who has travelled so much, how are you managing to keep the itchy-feet quiet?"

"When you travel so much, you want to feel that belongingness, to someone or someplace just so that you feel that you too have someone for you, who waits for you. Most people call that place home but home doesn't always need to be a place, it can be a moment, a person, or whatever that keeps you at peace."

"Maybe. Why did you visit all these places? I mean, everyone has their reasons. I just want to know yours."

"To feel home everywhere. Burn some in the sun, soak some in the sea, sink some to the sea-bed, float some into the air, throw a few into the sky. Spill your memories all over the world so that you feel at home everywhere you go. I just attempted that. My goal was to travel in a way that makes everywhere you go your own, place where you feel that its truly yours, something like, your grandma's home, the only place where we all can be what we are."

Robin is touching and feeling every photograph present there. "Boss, list out your top 10 favourite Indian travel experiences."

"Well, that is very difficult. I will give you a list but they're not in any order. These are the ten things that are coming to my mind, now. The next time you ask me the question, the answer might change."

"That is okay, boss. I just want to hear about a set of travel experiences."

XXV

"What are you concentrating on, so much for the last 30 minutes?" Anshul asked him.

"I'm preparing my last day mail Ass" Santhosh is still glued to his screen.

"You still have time; tomorrow will be your last day"

"Yeah, you will understand why I'm doing it now after reading it."

"Mention me in it, thank you. I'm the one who made your days beautiful in Pune, even in Nigeria, I helped you with a lot of things."

"Name some of those things."

"I told you where to eat Samosa, where to shop the useless stuff, where to waste your time effectively."

"Do you want me to mention all these?"

"You can shut up and just thank me in the mail."

Santhosh worked on his mail for over 45 minutes and dropped it right away. The mail read:

Subject: Sweets at my desk.

Body:

Dear Cyber labour,

Tomorrow will be the last day of my first job (if they don't throw me out today after reading this email). I hope this will be my first and last IT job. Every one of you, directly or indirectly are the reason for who I am today, and trust me, I deserve better than what I currently am. And it's not just me, a lot of us here deserve better than we are.

If there be,

Suggestions to seek,

Advice to add,

Questions to ask,

Clarifications to give,

Secrets to reveal,

Confessions to make,

Proposals to present (No way I'm getting these),

Curse words to pass (sure thing),

I'm here till tomorrow evening (Conditions apply). The only reason I'm dropping this mail a day early is, for all those people who might want to slap me but are planning to work from home tomorrow, I'm giving you all a chance today. Thank me later.

But before leaving, I want to quote Robin Sharma here, "Don't live the same day for 60 years and call it a life". Never give up on your dreams. There is always a way you can choose to pursue what you love.

Thank you all for supporting me in everything I did here. Special thanks to Anshul for being there for me always. (I've mentioned your name only because you asked for it, Anshul).

PS: There are no sweets at my desk, that was just a trap to lure you all into reading this mail.

If you are disappointed with this, you should have a look at your compensation letters.

#Be in touch:

Mail id: PleaseDonDisturbMe@gmail.com

Phone number: 797251XXXX (Person who be worthy will possess the power of those last 4 digits).

See you soon (just kidding),
Santhosh K

Christopher Johnson McCandless once said, "Careers are twentieth-century inventions, I don't need one". I believe in it.

Thanks,
Signing off.

His mailbox as well as his messenger app are flooded with the responses. From a lot of unknown people to the chiefs of different wings in the organisation responded.

A few of those responses stood out in which a girl said, "I am taking a print of this and keeping it in my cubicle as an inspiration" and another one from the financial chief read, "You seem to be a courageous man to take on the whole organisation. I wish you the best in your adventures. I am sure you would do adventures."

The mail stirred a lot of people. His Senior Project Manager said, "Cyber Labour?? Wrong choice of words. I didn't expect this from you."

"Labour is just the physical or mental effort put in by a person. So, what's wrong with the choice of words? We all put mental effort into the IT world and so, are cyber labour. I don't think there is anything wrong in admitting that we are labour." Santhosh responded to him to which there was no counter from his superior. Santhosh knew that there would be outrage about the mail as it is against a lot of expectations of the top layer people of the organisation. He indirectly attacked the complete system with a single-page mail. He came home that night with a lot of wishes and satisfaction which he couldn't get for all those years. A lot of people told him that his mail was a wake-up call for them. While there are a lot of people who feel frustrated every day but get grounded in the system and put on a fake smile felt good that someone took a stand to represent all of them, at least in the form of words. An unknown person met him to thank him, another one offered him the treat just as an act of gratitude and a lot more of these things happened. He understood that people always wait for someone to talk on behalf of them. It isn't common for someone to go against the flow, to express oneself completely impartially. He didn't know that he was doing something so special for people to admire him. He was just venting his frustration on the paper but didn't expect people to own it so much.

"So, you're not coming for lunch with us" Anshul turned to Santhosh.

"Nah, someone asked me out for lunch."

"Someone huh! you're becoming famous while leaving the organisation"

"The Dutch painter, Vincent Van Gogh became famous after he died. So, I guess this is a lot better comparatively."

"You don't always need to come up with heavy information. Silence is gold, remember."

"Shut up, I am getting late for my lunch date." "ha-ha, lunch date, I hope you don't fall asleep, loser."

Santhosh laughed. It's good to have someone who makes fun of your weaknesses. They are the people who constantly remind you that there is always scope for betterment.

Y

Pradeep took a leave from work for 2 days to be with Krish. He made it his priority to cheer him up at least a bit. Pradeep wanted to talk him out completely. When everything comes out, when there is nothing more left in for him to say, that would lessen the pain a little. It might free up some space inside the heart which is currently suffocating with a emotions. Pradeep woke him up so late and they went for a small ride and then, to the beach.

"I have been seeing your WhatsApp status posts and found them odd but then, you are always odd. I just thought that you were going through one of the phases but didn't expect it to come this far."

"Why did you bring me to the beach?" Krish is indifferent to everything these days. The beach used to be one of his favourite places. The top ten of his most favourite travelling places come with beaches and his dream destination, Maldives is an Island. Pradeep knew these and thought of getting him to a place where he would feel alive and fresh.

"Why? You like breaches." Pradeep replied.

"Beaches stir the mind. Not only do they take the sand away underneath your legs but also your strength by bringing back all the things that happened. The waves take away the sand and give you back the memories that burn you. Do you remember? You envied my ability to remember things for a long time but I promise you, it's not a boon mama. It's a curse to remember everything, including all tiny details. It is terrifying to remember everything, for long. To relive all the moments that hurt, to remember the scent of the people who broke us and recollect them at every moment when the slightest of the sparks related to them occur, even after decades into life. It makes it so difficult for someone to move on when one remembers everything."

Pradeep is learning a lot about handling a broken heart. All the things that were once considered good don't still need to be good. It all depends on your state of mind. It's called a heartbreak but it is more like a brain break. The brain doesn't work in its regular ways when someone experiences something so heartbreaking.

"And the Whatsapp status page is my chapel, that's where I confess" Krish confessed the reason behind all his status posts.

"Okay, and anyway, the beach stirred your memories. So, tell me why did she feel so suffocated in the relationship? What did you do so much that she had to break the bond to feel free?"

"Possessiveness."

"That's it? One word? No explanations. You blame me with a big explanation about what beaches do to you but one word for the reason why you guys broke apart?"

"She thought that I tried to change her, tried to change the way she lives. Not just a thought, She believed that I didn't like her the way she is. But I love her the way she is. I love the way she is so funny, so pretty, so childish and so lovely but then, I wanted all those to be mine, only mine. I wanted her greatest side known only to me. I wanted to be the only guy who makes her smile and the only person she turns to, for anything. I wanted her to be childish only when she is with me, to be so lovely only with me, and to be so funny only when we are together. I know it was selfish but isn't love selfish? I feel that there is nothing more selfish than love. I can't express how much I loved the way she is and I can't express how I wanted all of that only for me. Don't possessive people deserve love?"

"Hmm," Pradeep didn't want to answer that. He wasn't very sure either. "Did she mention that this was the case?"

"The best thing about her is she never lied. She did mention that it was making her uncomfortable. She named it differently though; she called it insecurity and she was right about that. Feeling insecure about someone might be the worst possible way of expressing that they mean the most to us but if you look at the brighter side of it, they mean the most. And we are insecure about someone when we know that they deserve better than us. The only way we can eradicate all their chances of getting someone better is by closing their doors, which generally results in restrictions. That doesn't mean we don't love them; we do and we are just scared of losing them. Scared of exposing them to any situation with chances of losing them."

"Coming to your earlier question, I don't know about the deserving part but may the possessive people be allowed to love but not the obsessive ones. Is love an obsession? But what do I know? Who am I but a single guy for life?" Pradeep is careful and stays on the diplomatic side with his arguments so that he doesn't hurt and provoke him much.

"Did you ever hear people in a relationship telling themselves something like, "You're mine"?"

Krish posed a question.

"Well, I don't remember listening to any of them in real life but did see that in a lot of movies and I guess people do express that to each other, at least during the earlier days of their relationship or marriage." Pradeep is now sounding serious.

"How does 'I own you' sound?"

"No one owns me" Pradeep was quick to react.

"Just imagine when a girl tells you, you're mine which sounds so romantic but if the same girl tells you that she owns you, that would make you think for a while, and all in a negative way, isn't it?"

"Maybe, but she has to take her time before saying anything because I would be in a shock for some time to realise the fact that a girl is talking to me." Pradeep is trying the funnier side of it.

"Not the time Pradeep, not at all."

"I'm sorry, most of these answers are designed, directed, and delivered by my Spine."

"So, you're mine sounds romantic but I own you sounds restrictive. Get your head around those statements, both are the same. You're mine is just as restrictive as I own you or I own you is just as romantic as you're mine. But that's not how we look at it. I don't know why. But honestly, I believe that love is an obsession."

"When our English teacher said that words and statements are important, I never thought that they are important for a relationship. I thought they were important just for those weekend tests." Pradeep told himself.

25

"Sitting on a cold aluminium bench outside Delhi airport during peak winter at 2 a.m. without a jacket, for 2 hours.

A roadside tea in Munnar, Kerala.

The quiet walk in the golden temple, Amritsar.

Visiting a gurdwara constructed on a hill which was elevated at 13000 ft, near Bumla Pass.

The serene forest-lemon water in the forests of Meghalaya.

Sharing the meals with Punjabi and Bihari regiment troops at the Madhuri Point in Arunachal Pradesh.

All the winter treks I have done in and around Pune.

A walk all along the coast of Pamban Island.

Hornbill festival of Nagaland.

Star-gazing at Mcleodganj, playing cricket with the locals in the Kashmiri valleys, enjoying the wine in Kasol.

As I already said, these are just a few of them that came to my mind, Robin."

"I want to do as many as I can, of all these. I want to do a lot more. I know that you've been to several other nations as well but I wanted the list of Indian experiences just so that I could try a few."

"Robin, I don't want to discourage you with any of the things you want to do. Try everything you want to do but remember, there will always be things that we want to do yet can't. But never define your life based on that. As long as you're not doing what you don't want to do, It's a beautiful life."

"We can't always do what we want to do but we can always not do what we don't want to do," Robin repeated. "That is one heck of advice, boss."

Both of them went mute and are in their own mind palaces thinking.

"Boss, if you don't mind me asking, did you ever get married?"

"No."

"Why? Is that something you didn't want to try?"

"No. I have been waiting for my next piece."

"Even now? after 60 years?"

"Yes."

"How do you believe in it, boss?"

"Energy is neither created nor destroyed. So, we are all just disintegrated, disoriented, and dispatched particles of the same matter. So, there can be a million pieces of me spilled all over the world. I found only one or two so far but there is always a chance for me to find more of them, any time, any day."

"For someone who travelled so much could only find one or two pieces, I wonder how much one needs to travel to find more."

"This is not a mathematical theorem to prove by taking a sample size, Robin. We never know, a lot of pieces might be just around for some and they must have been spread across

the world for someone else. But the most important part of it is, once you find one of those pieces, never let them go."

"But does it feel the same? I mean, to wait for someone or to fall in love with someone now?"

"No, we feel differently at every part of life, Robin. In teenage love, we live the moments, unaware and untouched by the thoughts of uncertain tomorrow, we stay in the present, that's why is it so beautiful? In adult love, you're always ahead of the time. You think of the life beyond, of a family. That is why anything after you cross 25, is difficult to lose, too hard to forget because tomorrow is always involved. Later, once you're 40, the hope diminishes but you should make sure of not giving in. There is no plan anymore after that, you just wait there for someone to come, and then, you take it from there. That is peaceful too."

"So, you are still courageous enough to love, again?"

"I don't know that but I'm sure stupid enough to do that again. Courage and stupidity are so close, both based on taking an uncertain risk. When you try something and if that works out, you will be called courageous and if that fails, you will be stupid. I am stupid enough to love again and fail again and I am courageous enough to be called stupid again. They all will live with me in the form of mental scars and that's okay. Physical scars are the proof that we survived and mental scars are the proof that we lived, invisible though."

Acharya sounded like a teenager and there was a long silence after that. Neither of them said a word. After a while, Robin re-kindled, "How do we find those pieces, boss?"

"You stand at a beach, all the waves, they look the same, they're all the same in fact but you have no idea which one will touch your feet. If you stand there long enough, one or the other side will surely reach you. The only thing is, you shouldn't run away."

As soon as Acharya finished the sentence, Srishti knocked on the door of Robin's thoughts.

He didn't want to open it but it did on its own. He knew that he needed to think further, he needed to figure out a way to have her in his life and not hurt her. He sat there quietly with his head in his hands. Acharya looked at him and he knew that Robin needed self-evaluation so, he left.

XXVI

Just like everyone else, Santhosh also has the same backup plan, home. Now, he's free from that everyday routine and is unaware of the next step, he wants to spend some free time. A time when he doesn't need to think about anything. He wanted to spend some quality time with his parents before letting them know what happened at work. After four days of relaxation, finally, the topic came up.

"So, when are you going back? Stay for another week at least. You haven't visited home in last two years" Mom said.

"There is something I need to tell you people"

"Who is that girl?" Dad joined the conversation.

"What girl? There is no girl"

"Then, what's that something that you wanted to tell" Mom is curious now.

"I quit the job"

"So, you will join another, right?" Mom is more curious now.

"No, I haven't given it a thought yet but I would like to change course. I don't want to do a similar thing again."

"What do you mean you want to change the course?" Dad is serious.

"I like travelling, I want to pursue something in that direction."

There was an uncomfortable, awkward silence for a long time. Dad is just staring at him without saying a word and Mom is sitting there like a doll, her face drained of blood. Both of them are shocked by his decision and neither of them are positive about that.

"This is something the rich do, to quit a job and pursue higher education or a business. We can't afford to do that." Mom is talking in a very low voice.

"That's the problem ma, the way we think. Why can only the rich have dreams? why can't we afford even a dream? Now, we have a house to stay in and brother has a job. He can take care for your needs till I figure out something. And I won't be depending on anything for my educational fee."

"If you're going to study again now, you will need another 2 years to finish it. Will you get a job right away after your education?"

"Maa, I haven't decided on the education yet. I will need to think it out. It takes some time for me to decide on which path to take."

"But if you start education now again, you'll need a lot of time to settle down again. When are you going to get married and when will you save some money for us? We neither get pensions nor have jobs. Who is going to fill my dreams?" Mom started the actual questions.

"Maa, I can't live these mundane lives, doing the same thing again and again on daily basis, staying at the same place and repeating the actions from morning to an evening like a machine. I am not a materialistic man; I can't think of your gold before taking a decision. I can only think of your health or your basic needs like food. That is all."

"Yeah, I see it. Your father didn't fulfil any of my needs and I can't even have my hopes on you."

"Maa, realise they are not your needs, they are wants. You don't need them to live. I love living a simple life, doing what I like to do."

"Okay"

All the above arguments didn't disappoint him as much as this "okay" did. She gave up the argument realising that there is no point in talking to him about this topic. But above all, he couldn't understand how gold matters to her so much, at the age of around 50. He understands that girls fancy it but even after leading a life for over 45 years and with kids, how can someone still worry about materialistic stuff and not about simplicity and happiness?

Probably, that's why a lot of families are unhappy. They are tangling their happiness with the status symbols, with the luxuries.

His dad kept quiet all this while and didn't utter a word.

"What are you thinking for so long Dad?"

"I have been calculating how profitable it would have been had I bought a couple of buffaloes 24 years ago."

Santhosh knew this, neither of them would take it easy. He talked to his brother and expected him to worry a bit as the responsibility on him increases but he didn't seem to care a bit. Perhaps, that's why his parents are worried.

A lot of things changed after that discussion. He isn't eating as much as he used to because he isn't as happy as he used to be. There aren't a lot of jovial conversations and when there are, they aren't smooth. Somehow, everything traced its way to the job, earnings, savings, and lifestyles. He wondered what kept his parents happy all these days, he wasn't ready to accept the truth. It wasn't him; it was his job that kept them happy. He waited for a quiet evening to talk to his mom.

"I don't think I am ready for marriage Mom, not in the next 5 years."

"Huh! Now, I've heard it all."

"I am not against marriage but I don't think I can live that life of sacrifices. Especially with all my dreams and targets online, marriage will just make it harder. And with no job, there is no way that I would get married, right?"

"So, you quit your job to escape marriage? We can postpone it if that's your plan."

"No, not at all. I quit because I wanted a different lifestyle. I love to travel, Ma. To meet new people, to live a different lifestyle every day, to understand different traditions, to eat different food, to see the sunrise from a different horizon each morning, to experience all kinds of climates, to visit remote villages and live their way of life, the diverse mindsets, cultures, beliefs, dressing styles, interests, stories, local history. I want to know all these, to understand how different we think we are but how common we are in our differences. Knowing there is a wide world out there and still being stuck at the same place makes me feel like an insect trapped in a spider web, aware of the danger yet unable to move."

"In a way, with all these things in mind, it's better not to drag a girl and their family into this. I was disappointed that all my hopes have been shattered but I understand it's your life and do what you want to do." Even though she didn't say it with all her heart, it was good enough for him to ease himself off that guilt. "But before deciding how to go ahead, keep it in mind that there are a lot of people who are just waiting to point at us. You take a turn from your regular life and try something new; their eyes light up. They wait at the corner to poke at you at every setback and we got a lot of those people in our family. So, whatever that you want to do, do it big. "

He knew she was right. He will need to figure out a way to sustain and then build a future. For all that to happen, he needs to figure out exactly what he loves to do. There are a few things he fancies doing. Reading books, travelling, writing stories and articles, reviewing movies, and making movies. In a nutshell, he likes to share his experiences or fantasies. He needs to do a lot of thinking to understand what he wants to achieve and needs to figure out a way to lead life in that direction.

Z

"Why are we in this place?" Krish is disgusted at the loud sounds and the bright lights all around him which are going dark quite frequently.

"Just for a change and for your kind information, this place is called a pub." Pradeep is his usual self, not seriously worried about his friend's situation.

"I know that this is called a pub, why are we here?"

"I already answered that question."

"But I hate pubs"

"I know and that's why we're here."

After learning that his favourite places are stirring back all the memories, Pradeep felt that he needs to get his friend a change of view.

"Care to explain?"

"I somehow feel that you're hating yourself more than you hate the fact of your breakup but whatever, I wanted you to forget that, at least for some time." Pradeep is very sincere with his answer.

"So, you brought me to a place that I will hate more than either myself or the breakup?"

"Spot on bro, that's why we're best bros."

Krish is just looking around still being disturbed by all the music. He always thought that he loves music but then, he realised that there is a good and bad side to everything, but then, it's his side of the coin again.

"So, decide what you want to hate most. Either the loud music or that guy there, the DJ who is playing it or the bartender who spilled a gin shot on you, or the big dance floor because of why all these people are here or hate all these people who are here on a weekday or hate your situation." Pradeep continued, "Only if I had these many options when I did my Under Graduation."

"I realised that I hate one thing more than all these."

"Hey, see, that's what I brought you here for. To understand yourself better. To discover things that you didn't know before."

"Yeah, thanks."

"By the way, what is that you hate the most now?"

"You"

Pradeep laughed and said, "Why are you shouting?"

"I thought you might lose my words in this absorbing music." He is taking a dig at everything.

"Okay then, I will be back after a dance." Pradeep disappeared into the crowd.

Krish sat there drinking his peg of whisky, looking around and wondering what makes them so happy and why they're all so different from him. Pradeep danced for over 20 minutes before coming back for another drink and was surprised by his friend who is submerged in his phone.

"Are you going to jump into that phone?" he asked Krish who had his phone so close to his face.

"I am finishing a poem that I wrote earlier."

Pradeep is happy to see his friend concentrating on something rather than burying himself in his sorrows.

"Ok, finish it. I will read it when I come back."

****

"Is this what you have been writing? I mean sitting in a pub with all the people enjoying the rock music, pretty girls dancing around and this is what you wrote?"

"It's not that bad," Krish answered in a very calm voice. Pradeep might have lost those words in that loud music.

U and I,

Not a regular girl and a guy,

U and I,

Lot more than what's visible to the naked eye,

U and I,

Look at each other and get high,

U and I,

We offer the sky a better night,

U and I,

Though tiny yet beautiful as a butterfly,

U and I,

Even without the wings, we can fly,

U and I,

Lots of laws of nature, we defy,

U and I,

As endless as the expansion of Pi.

U and I,

To the human world, a divine reply,

U and I,

Let's make this world a better place before we die.

U and I,

Without us, even the universe is a lie.

It's just a single verse without U n I.

This is the first part of the poem and that's not what Pradeep is reading. Krish just finished the second part of this poem and Pradeep got to read that.

U and I,
Met at a time when there were lots of knots,
U and I,
Are done even before we can start,
U and I,
Just as we named, are now stars apart,
U and I,
An unfinished yet complete art,
U and I,
Are at a point where we can't restart,
U and I,
Thankfully made some memories with the time we bought,
And now, that's all we got.
Maybe Only I,
Didn't ever want that love, to depart,
Maybe Only I,
Will suffer for offering my complete heart,
Maybe Only I,
Broke a lot of walls but all went to dirt,
Maybe Only I,
Need to rebuild an impenetrable fort.
But irrespective of where you are and what you do,
You're still my sweetheart.

Pradeep finished reading and he is furious.

"You are an idiot, an irresponsible one." Pradeep is shouting.

"Irresponsible? If you look around, I seem to be the only responsible guy in here." Krish is talking sense.

"There is nothing more irresponsible than being responsible here, this environment is created so that you can forget your responsibilities for some time. To ditch the common things for a while and submit yourself to the pursuit of happiness." Pradeep is scolding him now.

"Ditch common things? you mean common sense?" Krish's usual sarcastic self is gradually coming back.

"Do you think all these people are happy? Do you think happy people would end up in a pub on a weekday? I'm not suggesting that all people are sad or the people in a pub are sad but for the majority of people, entertainment is just an escape from reality and that's what I brought you here for. To skip reality." Pradeep sat down, "You deserve to be happy and you don't believe in that. It's time for you to start believing in it."

Krish knew Pradeep was right. But he still went ahead, "Is it you who is talking, or is it, Mr. Johnny Walker?"

"I didn't drink whisky, it was vodka" Pradeep is straight to the point.

"I'm sorry, I don't know why but I hate pubs. They just don't allow me to think."

"That's the whole point, Krish. Don't think and jump into unreasonable happiness. You think you are open to change but you're so scared of it. You can't even take a risk of dancing in a pub."

Krish knew that Pradeep is trying his luck at instigating him. Anyhow, he too wanted a change and to try dance. He finished his glass of whisky and went along with Pradeep to the dance floor.

26

"Robin, I can listen to those songs coming off your headset. Why is it on so high volume? Is that your favourite music?"

"Boss, didn't you ever use high-volume music just to keep your thoughts away?"

"Well, those times are in the past, Robin."

"I've something to confess, boss."

"So, are we going to a chapel?"

"Yeah, let's get on to the terrace." That's their chapel, that's where they confessed a lot of things to each other.

"I do love Srishti but I am way too scared to do anything about it."

"That is okay. The majority of our actions are based on fear, fear of losing something, of losing love, losing respect most people, fear of God. But we fail to feel the fear of losing self."

"But my past makes me so aware of everything that might come up."

"Never make someone in the present the victim of your past."

"But boss, after losing several people in life and even after being harassed by the memories of love, how can you ask someone to still go through the same?"

"Because it is worth it, Robin. We all need to send our love to the grave someday and then, what grows on top of it depends on our love, whether a jasmine spreading fragrance or thorns that keep hurting people around."

"We already had a lot of fights boss, it's like a broken mirror already."

"But it is still a mirror and you have it, a lot better than not having one," Acharya stressed.

"Aren't all relationships repaired? Do the successful ones not have any scars on them? They are all scarred, Robin and that's the best part of it, the scars are born by both of them and still could withstand the storms, and remember, they're all self-made storms, most of the time. Love is a constant fight with ourselves to let someone else in. Love is called a war, for a reason and to stress it again, it is the only war in the world worth fighting for."

"I don't know, boss. It sounds good when you ask me to do but when I think of it, it's a mess."

"Robin, I never ask you to do something, not when it comes to your life. You don't need to do something which others want you to do but make sure you're not brushing away something for that reason even when it's the right thing to do, there is nothing wrong in repeating something done by someone else when it is the right thing to do."

"But I feel like I'm losing freedom, boss. I feel suffocated in a relationship."

"Robin, love is like locking you in a cage and hanging you in the middle of a forest. As long as you're in, in your eyes, you think you're restricted of the freedom but in the other person's eyes, you're being protected from the predators outside." Acharya took a pause, "For the first time, I am telling you what to do. Talk to her, and explain your concerns. I don't think you ever did that." After asking him to talk to her, Acharya thought to himself, "Doesn't love give us the courage to lose a little freedom? Isn't it worth gambling a bit of freedom for love?"

"But, will it feel the same way? I mean, the magic of love."

"Just like you mentioned Robin, Love is like magic, once the trick is revealed, it is not interesting anymore. But to master it, it needs patience and when one has patience, everything else falls in place."

"Then, why do most of the love stories we hear fail?"

"Probably because most of them don't even understand magic."

"Okay, I am considering all your inputs but I've one last question."

"Shoot."

"Why did your relationship break?"

"While reviewing a self-work, we always rate it based on the effort we put into it but while rating others', we only consider the quality of the result. Process and efforts become immaterial. We failed to understand each other's efforts. We only considered the results.

Though I wanted to move ahead struggling, she didn't want it. She opted for peace over us, a fair choice maybe." Acharya paused a while, walking through the ancient roads of the past. "All the debris left after a breakup should be cleaned up by both but often, it's left to one person and it is too much for a single soul to handle. She never gave me a chance, if one is never given a chance to fix what they've broken, there will be two more broken things in the world."

"Can I just ask one more question, boss?"

"Yeah."

"What is the best and worst memory you've had with her?"

"It's the same moment, the last time when I met her."

"Did anything happen then?"

"When they leave and you stand there for that extra minute hoping that they would turn back, That's the hardest, slowest, deepest, and weakest minute of your life. But you know what, the best thing is when they don't turn back, that makes you the strongest, and then it's all upon you about how to make use of it."

"Make use of it?"

"Yeah, make use of the pain. Grief becomes fire and when it does, it either burns down the planet or lights it up."

XXVII

Days of calmness followed. Uncertainty started creeping in. Silence at home is so deafening.

All these days in his life, there was always someone who told him what to do. We think it's difficult to follow the advice and follow the steps of someone but that's the easiest thing to do. You will realise that once you're on your own when it's on your shoulders to decide what to make out of your life, that's the hardest. That's probably the reason why the majority of the world just repeats what their seniors have done, replicating similar lives. Now, at the juxtaposition, all his senses are freezing, and all the books he read aren't coming to his aid. Life seems to be rotating inside a bubble with no holes in it. Bouncing up and down inside the brain, he suddenly seems to be the master of mishandling life. But above all, he knew he couldn't quit, he needed to take control. The zeal to not stick to the same walls of the world is the only thing that stood alongside. Day after day, he is getting stronger gradually and unknowingly. He is learning to handle disappointments. There are few moments when he could sneak inside his brain for brief periods where he could think straight without being interrupted by the train of disturbing thoughts and he made the most of those moments. He sat and wrote down the things he enjoys doing in the order of priority and sorted out that travelling and story-telling are the two best things he prefers doing. So, either he chooses one of them or he needs to put them together. After a long time of over 13 days, which felt like months, he concluded that he is going to be a travel blogger, sharing all his experiences, and his stories. It includes everything he wanted to do; travelling, writing, and reading. Because he needs to find a way to monetize this, he wanted to do a professional course to understand how to make his stories reach a wider audience. And for that, he picked up two courses.

1. Masters in Fine Arts
2. Masters in Mass Communication.

Master in Fine Arts needs a bachelor's degree in Fine Arts as a prerequisite but the Mass Communication allows masters with a bachelor's degree in any stream. And so, his bachelor's degree in technology is helping him to do this. He then researched all the universities that offer scholarships and with the lowest fee margins as he needed to fund himself. He is not at an age where he can request and receive education fees from his parents and the education loans need collateral, so that's out of the equation too. With a lot of parameters to consider, he chose a public university to pursue the course and the course is called,

"Masters in Journalism and Mass Communication"

Now, the next important uphill task in front of

him is to convey this to his parents. He isn't waiting for their approval or support but he wants them to just accept that he is enjoying what he is doing. He is waiting for a moment to bomb them with the new shocking information. He applied for the entrance exam without informing them and with two days to the exam, while they were having dinner,

"I am going to do a master's in Journalism and Mass Communications."

They are all watching TV and no one concentrated on what he said and his whispering voice didn't help either.

"I decided what to do." He repeated.

"Is it any different from something which embarrasses and worries us?" his father sounded so sarcastic that Santhosh didn't even feel like continuing with the discussion.

"I am going to do post-graduation."

"Is that it? There got to be a twist in it. How can it be so normal?" his father is making it hard for him to go forward with the discussion.

"I am changing streams. I am not going to do a master's in technology, I am choosing arts this time."

"There you go", his father looked at his mother, "I knew, it cannot be so simple with him, he can't go with anything which isn't controversial. So, what art is it? Painting?"

"Journalism and Mass Communication."

"So, you want to be a journalist now?"

He knew that his parents would only concentrate on the 'Journalism' part and not on the 'Mass Communication' part. And it's more complicated because his actual interest is related to the 'Mass Communication' part.

"Nope, I want to be a blogger, to write stuff, to share stories. As I'm always interested in travelling, I would like to become a travel blogger or to work for any travel magazine. I may need to struggle for quite some time before I can get to do what I really want to."

"I can make only one thing out of all this. You're not going to earn anything any time soon."

"I cannot brush aside the possibility of that but it depends, If I can get a break soon, it would turn around in a very short time. But anyway, that is not what I'm aiming for. I want to do something I enjoy doing. I admit that I'm taking a risk, a huge one in fact, but I would regret it down the line if I don't do this now. We can't fake a thought. Once it's ignited in your head, there is no way you could ever turn it off, till the day you die. We can only brush it aside for the time being and then sleep with the regret every night or we should divert ourselves towards some pleasure. But I don't think I can ever do it. Once I decide to do something, I can never turn my back on it. Yes, I may not be able to earn for a long time but I can say one thing, I'll be happy. I prefer being happy struggling to regret every night on a cosy bed."

"Let him do what he wants to, he is trying something new. He anyway is not asking for any financial support from us. He is funding his education himself and there is no way you can say no to that." His mother came to his aid.

"As if I have a choice here. I am neither saying no nor saying yes. It is up to him." His dad left the room.

Neither did it go as well as he wanted nor did it go as worse as he expected. He is happy that it is over quickly. There are no more people whom he needs to persuade. Not needing to convince someone explaining what you do is right, is a pleasant feeling.

"I went against him to support you, make sure you do something worthwhile," his mother told him quietly with hope. Briefly, for a moment, he thought he was free but then again, those words from his mom put that pressure back on his shoulders.

ZZ

"I guess you need buttermilk or a strong lemon tea to clear off your brain a little" Pradeep shouted into the other room where Krish was searching for something.

"No, I am damn sure that I want to do this" Krish shouted back.

"Come here first and stop shouting"

"Wait, I am searching for my laptop."

"That is here, I have kept it on the table here. Come"

Krish entered the hall.

"Where is it?"

Pradeep slapped him.

"What the hell?"

"Now, are you still high? Do you need a couple more of them?"

"Prady, listen to me. I always wanted to do this and this might be the time for it. I now even have a reason and the data to go ahead. Believe me, I am not doing this for fame or fortune, but just to spread the things that I know might help someone someday. Even if it doesn't, it helps me and I have got nothing to lose too."

He didn't sound high or illogical and so Pradeep didn't have anything to counter him with.

"So, tell me where my laptop is."

"I don't know, I called you here just to slap you."

Krish went in again searching for his laptop.

"But what are you going to write in it?" Pradeep asked him.

"I thought about this last night while dancing mama. I will start explaining all the things I felt and everything I understood the exact way and where I finally ended up. I don't exactly know what she would have felt from her side but I know what I felt and that's exactly what I am going to write in the book."

Krish decided to compile a book with all his relationship experiences. Both his relationships are going to contribute to it, one from his Undergraduate days and the latest one, in post-graduation.

"I will write about all the pain I went through when I attended my girl's wedding a few years ago and how that changed my life for quite a long time before falling and failing in this again. I realised a few things that might help other people, so, I will just pass on the experiences and my feelings."

"Tell me a few things that you realised," Pradeep asked him sceptically.

"She always thought that I had problems with her past, with her ex-boyfriend but I never did. I only had problems when that past extended into the present which disturbed us. I couldn't handle that or convey that in a good way to her. I lost a few of my friends because of my inability to handle time management. And in a relationship, we often think that it ends with one discussion or a moment but that's not true, it happens gradually. With every fight, the distance grows, with every disagreement, the differences increase and they keep poking at you. Everything piles up and we fail to notice them. These are a few of the things that I realised, but very late. I will compile all these things that might help someone save their relationship."

"It is a very nice thought to begin with but why do you need to quit the course, your college? That would leave a huge scar on your career and that too, because of someone who is not going to be in your life. Do you think it is a good call?"

"I know it is not an ideal call mama but I don't have a choice. I can't grow in the same environment which breaks me every day. I love her and a lot of things she does might bother me, after what happened between us. I hate how she wants attention, not just mine, but everyone's. I hate how she wants to attend parties, the loud life. I hate how she used to forget herself amongst the crowds. But then, these are all my problems and they're going to bother me for sure. So, there is no other way, I need to get out of that campus, which is full of our memories. And about my career, I again don't have another option."

It's ironic to realise that people who don't deserve to break our careers are the ones who actually will do it.

"You regret it big time. Don't you?" Pradeep is concerned.

"Well, I regret meeting her, falling and failing in this relationship but I don't regret a single day I spent with her, the time we had, the memories of her sitting by me holding my hand. I always made fun of her loud voice but I wish I recorded that just to cherish now. I regret not doing that." Krish is turning emotional.

"You are not yet completely fine Krish, why don't you postpone writing this book?"

"I can't mama. The pen stops moving the moment the heart stops bleeding. There is no better time than this."

Pradeep is quiet. He understands that it is a deep cut and it will take some time to heal.

"I thought that my heart was as good as an ancient fort which doesn't have exits. But the heart isn't a fort and people can always find exits. Enemies might not be able to find out a way but the people who own it always can."

"Mama, add these lines to the book too. And, have you decided on the date to go back to the campus to get all your things?"

"Yeah, I will leave tomorrow. I will try to meet her one last time and end it on a good note so that I remember her face smiling. That's how I want to remember her, smiling."

"But won't that hurt you?"

"It won't be very different from how much it's hurting already."

"I understood one thing, mama. Tears aren't the only way to cry, some do cry in words."

"True."

27

Robin thought about all the events that happened in those last few months and has decided on taking action accordingly. The very next morning, he knocked on Acharya's room,

"Boss, I am going to talk to Srishti and will take it further depending on how things turn out there."

Acharya is happy to hear that but as always, isn't failing to use the situation.

"What happened to 'she deserves better'?"

"Well, she does but she deserves me too. That is what I am going to tell her and then, it's her choice."

Acharya smiled.

"I am leaving my books here, placing them in the shop but only for reference and not for sale."

"I will take care of that. But what about your pay for this month? Shall I send it at the end of the month over a courier or do you want to clear that out now?"

"Let us have some unfinished business, boss.

Sometimes, it feels so good not to be measured. Whenever they pay you, it's like a sealed deal but when they don't and you smile at each other and move on, there is that unfinished bond between the two. That feels magical, probably that is magic."

"Compassion is one of those magics, Robin." Acharya went inside to bring something, "Here, take these."

Robin looked at the books Acharya handed him and was surprised to see his boss's name on them. "You authored a book?"

"Well, yeah. The first time I wrote this, I finished it quickly but then, it took me a few decades to amend it. Over time, after every passing year, I learnt more and more about handling love and now, I feel I can pass it over to you, to the next generations. Read this because you remind me of myself and if possible, give the other copy to her. If it helps you keep your relationship, I would be glad."

"Boss, you are fabulous. As a reader, I understand it is not easy to write a book. I wish I could write one, someday." The young and excited blood of Robin is talking.

"You might, someday. Just like there is a sculpture in every stone, there is a writer inside everyone. Stone just has to go through enough pain to get the sculpture out."

Robin came with a stack of books and left with one book in hand, two copies of the same one.

XXVIII

He never thought he would ever do a post-graduation but that's how things turn out, life makes you dance to its tunes and you oblige.

It's been very long since he appeared for any entrance test. The last time he did was 10 years ago, for his engineering seat. It's a strange feeling to sit with a lot of younger people, take the same test, and be judged by the same questions while you're already 5 years older and a bit more experienced. It didn't seem fair to him but there was nothing he could do.

Just like every time, he is early into the examination hall waiting for everyone. It isn't a good thing to get to your examination centre way early because that gives you a lot of time to think and then, there are a lot of things that come to mind, especially the ones that shouldn't. Strangely, he started thinking about the movies that he watched recently, his top playlist of songs, and all his favourite cricket games as if he were sitting on a riverbank and enjoying the sunset. He completely forgot that he is in an examination hall. It started filling in and it felt as if the seats inside a movie theatre are being occupied. 30 minutes later, he is handed the question paper and the marking sheet in which he started mentioning the details.

Name: N Santhosh Krishnan
Hall Ticket Number: A19100SS011
Course: Social Sciences

ZZZ

"I'm waiting at the same place, the place where Us started and where it ended." Krish texted her. They decided to meet for one last time just for the old time's sake.

"Wait, I am coming, won't be long."

Krish sat there thinking how he liked a few of her perfect imperfections but never realised them.

"Hey," Prags is there in her regular wear, torn jeans, and a tee. He noticed them right away but there was nothing he could say about it anymore and he knows it. "Why are you leaving? You should complete the course. I am behind it, Aren't I?"

"Hey, nothing of that sort. I have nothing more to get from here except for the certificate. But you know, I am not someone who cares about certificates."

"Yeah, but there is no reason for you to leave in the middle of the course too, right? Except for us moving apart."

"That is one way to look at it. But yeah, I can't move on as long as I stay here. Need to get out of this place to get it out of my head."

"Hmm." That reply from her hurt him a little, to realise that she cares only as much. "Okay then, it was good while it lasted. See you again, sometime later when you're better."

"Sure." He couldn't manage to say anything more. That is going to be a long time before he would get to see her again. As soon as she stood up, he is about to say "Love you", which has always been their way of saying bye but he stopped himself from doing that. She left and got in the car while he waited there till it went out of sight wishing she would turn back one last time just like she used to do. That hurt him a little more. He knew he wouldn't be able to move on completely ever. He will never forget that moment. With every broken relationship, there is a little hole that is left inside the heart that can't be filled by anything, and right then, we bring in art like poetry or music to fill those voids, at least temporarily.

As soon as she left, he texted Pradeep, "We met and she just left."

Pradeep replied "Forget about that. Actually, I didn't admit it then but I liked that reference of Pi in your poem. I loved it." He tried to get his friend out of that self-pity zone.

"A true math-lover," Krish responded.

That night, Krish embarked on writing his book and it went like this.

Those eyes, they are the most dangerous. More than the breakup, the question of her love troubles me more, whether she really loved me or just used me. But the moments we had, the time we spent, the way she looked at me, all those felt beautiful and genuine. But is this how they do it? I believe that the most dangerous people are those who can lie with their eyes.

He finished writing the book over 8 months and named it,

"A MILLION PIECES"
By N Santhosh Krishnan.

28

"Is everything fine?" Srishti is genuinely worried.

"I know I don't do this but yeah, let's meet in the evening."

They chose the nearest beach as their meeting spot. Robin reached the location early to decide and practise how to go on with the conversation. Meanwhile, Srishti is searching for him all along the coast and finds him at a distance, mumbling to himself.

"Is everything fine?" she asked him the same question again.

"Yeah, I guess...guess." Robin is stuttering. "Everything is fine but I have a feeling that they are going to get better."

Srishti's hopes rose like a big wave. As an experienced lover, she knew not to expect a lot but she didn't know how not to. It is almost like competition between the tides of the ocean and the strides of her expectations, a competition where who rises higher and who falls heavier. She just stood there quietly for him to finish talking.

"As you're a science student, let me speak your language. Oxygen is a supporter of combustion but if you mix it with hydrogen which becomes water, is a fire extinguisher. That's what a partner or a bond can do to you. They can change you completely and mould you or they might just complete you."

Srishti is emotionally ecstatic but mentally stuck. She didn't know how to react to something like that, which she never expected.

"But you said you're not like everyone and you can't stick to democracy and a lot more stuff which I generally ignore."

"You ignore?"

"Yeah, once I realised that you're saying a no, I couldn't listen to the rest of it."

"Feelings aren't democratic Srishti, they are mostly revolutionary. Truth is mostly on the side of the minority. So, yeah, I am not a democratic social friendly person but the truth seems to be on my side." Robin took a deep breath and put his hand around her shoulder, pulling her a little closer. Still looking at the setting sun and the rising waves, he said, "I love you".

Srishti didn't say a word.

"I never knew that a departure of a day can be so beautiful too."

He then pulled out the book he received from Acharya and gave it to her.

"Read this. We were gifted these by my boss from work."

The book was titled, "A Million Pieces" by Acharya N Santhosh Krishnan

Neither Acharya nor Robin knew whether he would be able to handle the relationship but he was courageous enough to give it a try, that is all one can do and that is all one needs to do.

Try.

www.ingramcontent.com/pod-product-compliance
Lightning Source LLC
LaVergne TN
LVHW061544070526
838199LV00077B/6894